Security Decisions

Executive Summary

The CISO Toolkit is designed as a toolkit for the Chief Information Security Officer (CISO) of a substantial enterprise. This is "Security Decisions", a decision support tool for the CISO that actualizes many of the notions underlying the Toolkit in a standard form that allows specific decisions to be made quickly and with a solid basis.

This decision support tool includes a series of articles, each designed to address a specific decision that is commonly made by an enterprise. For each decision, there are five parts:

- **Issue:** The issue is codified into a simple question that the article is intended to answer.
- **Options:** Each question has a set of typical options for resolving the issue at hand.
- **Decision:** The decision indicates under which circumstances each option should be taken. This maps the issues into the options and results in a decision.
- **Basis:** Every decision has a basis in reason. The basis section describes why the decision is made as it is and under what circumstances these reasons may not apply.
- **Summary:** The summary concludes the article by reiterating the basic points, what had to be decided, why, and how it was decided.

Each decision is done in two pages, making these articles ideal for executive decision-making and presentation to top decision makers. These articles are also commonly used to explain decisions, as leverage when a decision without a sound basis comes to the CISO, and as a means to explore other options when a decision has been made without adequate consideration.

At the end there is a section for writing down the current situation and the decisions made for the desired situation relating to every issue identified ion the book. There is also a one-page description of the market space for security-related tools and support intended to track the general areas in which there is no help, inadequate help, reasonable and appropriate help, and too much competition to be really helpful. The CISO ToolKit is intended to address the top two rows of that chart.

Finally, a set of blank pages are left at the back for your notes.

Front Matter

The CISO Toolkit - Security Decisions - 2006
is copyright © 1977-2006 by Fred Cohen, all rights reserved.

Published by ASP Press and Fred Cohen & Associates out of Livermore, CA.

ISBN: 1-878109-38-3

LICENSE:

Table of Contents

Improving security: What's a good first step?

Issue:

What is a prudent first step I should take to improve my corporate information security program?

Options:

Options include; (1) do a rapid risk assessment, (2) do a protection posture assessment, (3) do an external information technology audit, (4) do nothing.

Decision:

For small businesses, option 1, a rapid risk assessment using an outside expert firm is advised. For medium sized businesses that are privately held, option 2 is a better option as it is more thorough and reasonably affordable. Option 3 is essentially mandatory for any publicly traded company, but many such companies also engage in option 1 or 2 for select new implementations and for annual external validation of their protection processes. In all cases, it is necessary that an independent outside expert or organization be engaged in this activity just as in a financial audit. Option 4 is only viable if you have already taken the first step and it tells you to go no further or if you have little or no information technology dependence.

Basis:

Risk management is the core process underlying all prudent decisions about information protection. In order to make prudent decisions, a risk management process must be put in place, and the first step is an independent assessment.

The least expensive and simplest first process in understanding business risks associated with information technology is a rapid assessment. One or two reasonably expert people can do a rapid review of business and information technology issues for a small company in one or two days on site, followed by a day or two of writing up what was found and what it means, and a short review by a second expert to assure that the report makes sense. This typically costs between $17,000 and $27,000, is scheduled a few weeks in advance, and produces a 15--25page result with a list of obvious changes that make sense. With this much time and effort, the task can not be done very thoroughly and individual expertise of the person visiting the site is especially important. Expect them to ask all sorts of questions about your business, because it's the only way they can learn enough in a day to understand what's most important.

The next step up the assessment ladder is an information protection posture assessment. These processes involve site visits by several skilled people for a few days, and include a variety of scans for vulnerabilities, discussions of business issues, technology reviews, physical reviews, and an assortment of other similar processes. After a few days on site, the team goes back, analyzes for a few weeks week about the situation, and writes up a document of about 40 pages with short, medium, and long-term recommendations. Expect to pay between $35,000 and $75,000 for a protection posture assessment and to gain a very good understanding of what it will take to move toward a strong long-term information technology risk management process.

The third option is for those with a more substantial budget and a great desire to get a lot of details over a period of a few months. This sort of external audit will be a real eye-opener, but if risk management processes are not already in place in one form or another, it may be too much to bear. In these cases a team of people with different skill levels will be unleashed upon your business and do detailed reviews of system after system, going over extensive checklists, and generating reports that can range up to hundreds of pages or more. Expect to pay at least $125,000 for this audit and expect it will take many months to make a substantial portion of the changes they suggest. Don't expect it to help you form an improved risk management process, because these sorts of efforts are really about delivering thousands of action items at a detailed level for those that are trying to eliminate as many faults as they can identify. As a first step such an audit may provide too much detail leading to attempts to defeat vulnerabilities at a detailed level and providing potential ammunition to lawyers wishing to bring suit for negligence for failure to fix everything found. A sound risk management foundation is the key objective of these first steps.

Many companies make the mistake of hiring a relative or friend for assessment processes. Some of these processes can be effective, while others may not be, but there is an important issue that these approaches fail to address. Unlike employees, relatives, and friends, a well qualified, independent outside expert will tell you the straight truth as an outsider would see it. They will be untainted by allegiances, friendships, or other ties that tend to soften harsh truths or take into account internal political viewpoints. A prudent first step in information protection is always predicated by eliminating any motives or allegiances to anything but the things you need to know.

Summary

Depending on the time, money, and outcomes desired, each of these three common assessment processes can be effective at helping to get a proper protection environment set up for your business. The thing they all have in common is that independent outside experts are used to make the process work.

Defining risk: How should I define risk levels?

Issue:

What is a reasonable way to define risk levels for my protection program?

Options:

Options include; (1) analyze everything in terms of financial numbers, (2) use a 3-level system with low, medium, and high risks defined, (3) use a 10-level system rating risks from 1 to 10, (4) don"t rate risks.

Decision:

For most businesses, option 2 is suitable as a top-level discriminator and since people tend to work better with fewer levels, it works almost all of the time. Option 3 is used by companies with highly advanced risk management programs when there is justification for ten different protection profiles and ten different levels of countermeasures are well defined. Option 4 is fairly commonplace but it is a bad idea and for public companies in the US, it is not within the bounds of the law. Option 1 sounds good but it is in fact hard and expensive to do and ineffective in application because it does not lead to utility in terms of defining defenses.

Basis:

Option 1 uses probabilistic risk assessment (PRA) or a similar system to derive financial metrics that codify expected losses and event sequence probabilities so as to generate expected loss. Defensive measures are then applied to reduce expected loss. The problems with this approach are many, including high cost of the undertaking, inability to accurately codify everything in terms of numbers, difficulty with using probability distributions and confidence intervals instead of fixed numbers to mitigate the inaccuracies with fixed values, sensitivity defense selection to minor changes in values used in computations, and inability to list all event sequences of interest. In fact, even the losses associated with events after they take place are often hard to agree on to within several orders of magnitude.

Option 4 is problematic in that it fails to address the basic need to systematically address risks. The Sarbanes-Oxley act mandated that all public companies undertake to understand and describe business risks internally and to their shareholders, and this notion is sweeping the world as a mandatory component of any rational business management. Executives can go to jail for failing to properly understand and report risks to shareholders, and certainly any rational business owner wants to understand risks and deal with them prudently. For this reason, option 4 should not be used.

Option 2 is a 3-teir system for codifying broad levels of risk. Typically:

- **Low risk** is defined as anything that is similar in consequence to a slip and fall accident, anything that normal business insurance standardly covers, and day-to-day office issues.

- **Medium risk** is defined as things that cause substantial negative publicity, partial loss of business, losses in the range of 5% or more of annual revenues, legal difficulties for officers, workers, or others, things that interrupt production or cause quality control problems in important manufacturing systems, and other similar sorts of events that don't reach the level of high risk but are not in the range of normal every day things.

- **High risk** is defined as things that can put the enterprise out of business, cause large-scale loss of shareholder value, cause significant damage to the environment, cause governmental agencies to stop doing business with you, cause loss of life, get officers thrown into jail, or result in other very serious negative consequences.

This is advantageous because it is relatively simple and because it allows defined protection measures to be used for the different risk levels without undue complexity and while reasonably addressing the basic needs. More detailed system-specific protection measures are also needed in many cases, but this is a good starting point.

The 10-tier system, or other similar systems with large numbers of levels present advantages and disadvantages. The advantage is finer granularity of control and less bunching of wider ranges of things together. The disadvantage is complexity of understanding and management. For example, there are rarely well codified procedural differences between tiers 6 and 7, different HR requirements, different legal requirements, and so forth. This means that some thiungs change with tiers and some things don't, which makes the system harder to manage and operate. Systems also tend to move from tier to tier more often when there are finer differentiations and people tend to argue over the subtle differences. Another major problem is that there aren't usually ten different levels of surety for protective approaches to any given issue, so the minor differences in the tiers don't result in substantial changes in how things are protected.

Summary

All enterprises should rate risks and risks associated with information technology are reasonably rated with the 3-tier system used throughout the CISO ToolKit books. For highly advanced risk management programs, a 10-tier system or other process is reasonable, but PRA is problematic in most cases.

Spam: How should I handle it?

Issue:

What is the right combination of technical, procedural, and other approaches that should be taken to minimize spam email entering my business without otherwise having a negative effect on our operations?

Options:

Six options are readily available for countering spam. (1) Remove individual employee email addresses from web sites and similar public areas. (2) Refuse to accept email from large-volume spam sources. (3) Scan incoming email for known spam content and remove it. (4) Select an ISP that has good spam blocking as part of their service. (5) Commercial antispam solutions are available. (6) Refuse to forward spam email. (7) Don't allow internal email lists to work from external sources.

Decision:

We advise a combination of all seven elements as part of your antispam effort, with increasing application of these methods with increasing spam issues. Option 1 should be standard practice for most businesses. Option 2 is problematic unless you have an alert systems administrator or use an antispam service. Option 3 is necessary for almost all businesses. Option 4 is good if technical skill is lacking, or if ISP spam blocking is desired and available. Option 5 should be used if no internal expertise is available. Option 6 should be used in all cases. Option 7 should be used by all enterprises especially when mailing lists with addresses like "everyone" or "all" are in place and a single spam email can reach all of the workers.

Basis:

Spam is unwanted and unsolicited, typically commercial, email. It is sent in sufficient volume to become a hindrance to business and employees, and it can be harassing, abusive, suggestive, or solicit illegal and unbusinesslike activities. Spam is now estimated to consume far more than 1/2 of all email received by most companies. Reduction and elimination of spam email is becoming a necessary part of most businesses who use email as a major means of communication.

Spammers tend to farm the Internet for addresses to add to their spam lists. By not listing employee email addresses on web sites and similar public forums, their addresses will be harder to find and you will get less spam. If email addresses are widely published already, consider changing email addresses of employees and providing automatic responses to update legitimate contacts as to the new addresses. White lists can also be used to allow known email contacts to continue to use the old email addresses during the transition.

Much, but not most, of today's spam comes from a relatively small number of high volume spam sources. These ISPs make their money by selling bandwidth to spammers. By refusing email from these domains as your email gateway administrator detects them and notifying the sources of these emails of the reason for the refusal, you will reduce the business value of these spammers while eliminating a significant portion of all the spam you receive.

Spam tends to come in large quantities with related subjects and content. Much of this spam is easy to detect by watching as new spam comes up and adding lists of words to content-detection filters. Similarly, a lot of spam comes from foreign countries in text formats that are unique to those countries. By filtering on character sets a lot of spam can be rapidly eliminated. For example, "charset=gb2312", "Worm.Sobig", "details.pif", and "Viagra" are all very popular terms in spam today. For more extensive lists, there are services that help identify the patterns most commonly used in spam.

If you control your own email gateway, make sure to configure it so that it doesn't forward spam by eliminating forwarding from sources not within your own domain. Also, eliminate address forgery and similar tricks that allow spam to masquerade as being from you. Eliminating external access to internal lists prevents the use of "all" or "everyone" as addresses that forward the spam throughout the enterprise along with many of the replies. If you use an ISP for your email, find an ISP that does a good job of reducing spam and not sending out spam to others. If you ask the ISPs they will tell you what they do.

Commercial antispam solutions are widespread. They are also now integrated into many email clients for free and should be used when available as they have almot no cost and are reasonably accurate.

Summary

Spam can be largely reduced or eliminated by some relatively simple tricks of the trade. These are excellent first steps, and in most cases, they will be good enough to reduce the problem to tolerable levels for your business.

Spyware: How should I handle it?

Issue:

What is the right combination of approaches to reduce spyware in my business without otherwise having a negative effect on our operations?

Options:

Five options are readily available for countering spyware. (1) Move away from Windows on the desktop. (2) Ignore spyware for low consequence systems and focus on medium and high risk systems. (3) Block spyware at a gateway device. (4) Block spyware on Windows desktops. (5) Disable Windows functions that spyware exploits.

Decision:

If feasible and spyware is a significant concern, we advise option 1. It is highly, semi-permanently, and immediately effective. Option 2 is reasonable if a proper protection architecture is in place to determine which systems are of low enough consequence to ignore spyware issues. Option 3 is effective at reducing spyware to a relatively minor issue but should not be used for medium and high risk situations. Option 4 is good for businesses with highly mobile information workers that connect to networks from wherever they are. Option 5 sounds appealing but the things that have to be disabled are most of the most widely used things in the Windows environment and not all of them can be completely disabled.

Basis:

Spyware is a name given to the increasing number of Trojan horse software elements that have been launched predominantly by commercial and criminal interests to gather personal data on individuals and businesses. These software fragments are used by those who set them on the world for activities ranging from stalking of individuals, to gathering illicit corporate intelligence, to industrial espionage. Spyware is estimated to be present in more than 80% of all corporate Windows platforms but it is almost nonexistent in any other platform because of a combination of factors. Reducing or eliminating the consequences of spyware is becoming a necessary requirement for many businesses because of potential liability for the information leaked, negative publicity, and regulatory concerns.

Spyware, like computer viruses and other malicious code and remote attacks, is predominantly created to work in the Windows environment that dominates the desktops of major corporations and end users. The solution of moving from Windows to OSX (Apple's operating environment) or Linux is very cost effective not only because of spyware defense costs but because it reduces or eliminates the need for antivirus software and other similar defenses. While the day may come when other platforms are targeted, the annual security maintenance cost for the typical Windows computer today (commonly estimated to be about $1000) is more than the cost of acquiring and operating the typical Apple or Linux computer. Both of these platforms support Microsoft formats and have desktop applications comparable or identical to Microsoft's. Both also offer remote desktop to allow a small number of Windows Citrix servers to support Windows-only functions from user workstations running these operating systems.

Reducing Windows functionality to reduce spyware includes removing or disabling Internet Explorer, Word, PowerPoint, Excel, and Outlook as well as disabling ActiveX. But these are the very reasons people use Windows computers in the first place. This is an infeasible solution for user desktops but it is feasible for Windows servers and should be undertaken.

Ignoring spyware for low consequence systems and focus on medium and high risk systems for spyware defenses saves a lot of money but requires an effective security program that differentiates these systems based on the factors relevant to the spyware issue.

Blocking spyware at a gateway device is highly effective for risk reduction to acceptable levels in most enterprises however it does not cover mobile workers very well. Blocking spyware on Windows desktops for mobile devices is effective at risk reduction, however, the hidden maintenance costs are very high in cases where users manage their own spyware solutions and centralized management for mobile workforces is expensive and requires integration of spyware defenses into existing security management systems. In these cases selection of a spyware protection vendor should be based on what is already supported within the enterprise for centralized management because there is little discernible quality difference between vendors and the cost of operation and maintenance far overshadows price differences between products.

Summary

Spyware and many related problems can be eliminated by moving to Apple or Linux user platforms while reducing computer life cycle costs and staff requirements for information security. For those who cannot or will not make such a move, spyware cannot be completely eliminated but it can be reduced at the cost of more security maintenance and overhead using commercial products. Product selection should be based on what fits the enterprise architecture and not based on properties of the specific offerings, which are essentially indistinguishable from a technical standpoint.

Wireless: How should I handle network access?

Issue:
What are the options for making wireless access safe within my business environment?

Options:
Options include: (1) don't allow wireless access, (2) put wireless access on separate firewalled network segments, (3) use Wired Equivalent Privacy (WEP) or Wi-fi Protected Access (WPA) to secure wireless, or (4) treat wireless access like remote access.

Decision:
Option 1 is an outstanding choice but may be difficult because wireless access has many beneficial properties including convenience and ease-of-use. Option 2 is a necessity if wireless is to be used at all. But this limits the effectiveness of wireless and increases its cost. Option 3 uses encryption and authentication, which is better than operation without encryption or authentication. Option 4 is the best option for most businesses and can be combined with Option 3.

Basis:
Wireless can be compelling because of the convenience and reduced wiring costs associated with its use. The problems with wireless are that it is highly susceptible to disruption, surveillance, corruption, and unauthorized use. These problems can only be countered with additional authentication, encryption, and physical security, which in turn eliminate much of the convenience and increases the costs. As a result, the advantages of wireless are largely offset by its security limitations except in select environments.

Disallowing wireless should be considered for environments where wireless is not needed and no obvious cost savings are to be found. Many businesses can now make a legitimate case for the cost savings and improved operational efficiency for their mobile workforce and their on-site guests, but only if the implement wireless in a highly reliable manner. Typically, wireless that really works throughout a facility and is properly secured costs on the order of $1 per square foot, far more than the cost of simply putting wireless access points at a variety of places within a building.

Putting wireless access on separate firewalled network segments is a sound practice. It protects other areas of the network from the wireless systems, but in exchange these systems don't have access to the rest of the network, and of course the wireless systems may be vulnerable to each other. As more of the business goes to wireless, the risks increase. The cost of additional firewalling is not substantial, typically on the order of less than $200-$2000 per network segment. Firewalls can also limit access based on MAC address and augmented authentication, can be used to enforce the presence of specific controls, and can require proper encryption and keys or certificates for connectivity.

In option 3 either WEP or WPA encryption is used to improve wireless security. Unfortunately, WEP is very common and inexpensive to use but also very weak. There are freely available tools on the Internet to break into systems running WEP, so it is only effective against people who are novices. In other words, it is nearly useless as a security tool. WPA seems for the moment to be far more secure, but in exchange a lot of additional effort is required to manage the encryption system and authorization mechanisms. Unless a high quality network-wide identity management solution is in place, this is problematic.

If the wireless network segments will be granted access to the rest of the business network, option 4 and 3 combined is called for. Option 4 is the best alternative for wireless protection. In this approach, wireless users are treated like users from the Internet. The same protection measures to protect the internal networks against unauthorized remote access over the Internet are used for protection against the users on the wireless network, so the network is no more threatened from the wireless network than from the Internet. And of course the wireless users will need protection for their systems equivalent to the protection they would need if out on the Internet, so they will be usable on the internal wireless networks or from the Internet in the same manner. While the costs may be substantial, most wireless users are also using laptops, personal data assistants, or similar technologies that are mobile. They take these technologies on the road or home anyway. So the costs required for that use is leveraged for internal wireless use as well.

The use of option 3 with option 4 provides an added layer of encryption which is a good idea for otherwise unencrypted traffic. For example, when secure socket layer (SSL) encryption is used for Web-based connectivity, there is little if any advantage to using WPA to enhance it, but on the other hand, adding WPA doesn't typically degrade operations and adds a layer of protection for non-encrypted traffic.

Summary

No wireless system is effective against malicious service disruption by skilled and resourced attackers dedicated to disrupting services. However, if wireless users are firewalled from the internal networks and treated as if they were users from the Internet, wireless can be safely and effectively used within most businesses for non-critical functions.

Firewalls: What kind should I use?

Issue:

Does my network need a firewall, and how should I configure it?

Options:

Options include; (1) no firewall is used, (2) a network address translation (NAT) firewall is put in place, (3) a demilitarized zone (DMZ) area is used for servers, (4) multiple firewalled areas are used to separate areas from each other, and (5) personal firewalls are placed on select computers. Options 2, 3, 4, and 5 can be combined.

Decision:

We strongly advise every Internet connected company against option 1. In most cases, option 2 should be used for connections from company sites and the Internet. The firewall should use NAT to separate internal systems from direct Internet access. Networks supporting externally accessed servers should also use option 3, a DMZ, for those servers. If there are high-valued networks they should also be firewalled using option 4. Finally, if there are wireless or open access networks, they too should be firewalled, with all systems connected to those networks implementing option 5, personal firewalls. Expect to pay anywhere from $1500 to $10,000 for an option 2-4 firewall and proper installation, depending on the desired functionality. In some cases firewalls can save a lot of money on Internet service fees and in reduced costs of attacks. Personal firewalls (option 5) are free under Linux, Unix, and Apple OSX operating environments or can cost as much as $100 each for Windows-based computers. They must also be managed.

Basis:

Firewalls often seem like unnecessary pieces of equipment that cost a lot and do little, but modern firewalls do quite a bit to protect a network from external attack, and they are inexpensive for the protection they provide. If they are not properly configured, they may be ineffective and provide only a false sense of security.

With only the rarest of exceptions, companies need to firewall internal computers from the Internet. The cost of a firewall can be as little as a few hundred dollars, but you should also count on installation and configuration costs, maintenance costs, and the need to alter functionality to meet changing business needs.

The simplest and most common firewall technique is called NAT. In NAT one external IP address is used to allow an unlimited number of internal machines to access the Internet. This lowers ISP fees in many cases by reducing the number of IP addresses required for the business. It also prevents direct attack on internal computers and allows changes of ISP to be done more quickly and easily than would otherwise be possible. By translating all internal traffic into a single external IP address, attackers cannot directly reach internal computers, and this means that most Internet worms and other direct attacks will fail. For a qualified vendor to purchase, install, and configure this simple sort of firewall properly for a 100Mbits/second interface costs about $1500 and takes only a few hours of on-site time. Internal addresses will have to be changed at installation, but after that, they can remain the same regardless of changes by your ISP.

For networks supporting external servers, a third connection to the firewall is used to form a DMZ where externally accessible machines reside. The firewall can limit access to DMZ machines so that only authorized external services appear on the Internet. Different services reach those machines from internal addresses for maintenance and update processes. If access to back-end servers is required, this can also be allowed on a limited basis from the DMZ so that even a successful attack on a Web server will only grant limited access to internal networks. A qualified security vendor should be able to purchase and properly install this sort of firewall for between $2500 and $4000 and do so in a day or two, depending on the complexity of the situation.

Many companies have high valued internal networks that should be protected against internal users who are not authorized to access them. This is common for companies with data centers that support mainframe applications or wish to keep management and bookkeeping systems, marketing systems, research and development systems, health insurance systems, and production floor systems separated from each other. In these cases internal firewalls are often called for. Each internal firewall might cost $2500 to $5000. This may take a few days for a vendor to implement, depending on complexity of the previous situation.

Wireless or open access networks are problematic. They should be firewalled, but the effectiveness of these firewalls is limited if users use the mobility provided by wireless to do their work from anywhere in the company. A reasonably effective wireless firewall can be implemented for most companies.

Summary

Firewalls are critical and effective protection elements for most companies. They are imperfect but cost effective ways to limit direct attacks and control access. They require expertise to configure and maintain. As a matter of due diligence, and as a cost and consequence limiting measure, firewalls are highly advised.

Concealed networks: When should I use them?

Issue:

When is it appropriate to use deceptions to defend my networks and systems?

Options:

Options include: (1) never use deceptions, (2) use deceptions when they are built into existing systems, (3) use deceptions at firewalls, (4) use deceptions within internal networks, and (5) use deceptions within systems.

Decision:

Option 1 is infeasible because essentially every system uses deception in one form or another in its defenses. Option 2 is the most commonly used option because there is no added cost or effort. We advise the use of option 3 and option 4 when they help detect and respond to event sequences with potentially serious negative consequences. Option 5 is not a well developed technology area yet and we advise against its use except in high risk situations when adequate expertise is available for effective implementation and use.

Basis:

Deceptions increase the cost and complexity of attack for attackers while decreasing the effort required to detect, delay, and counter attacks. But deceptions also have some costs associated with their operation. Deceptions are good business decisions when the benefits outweigh the costs.

It is infeasible to never use deceptions for defense. For example, almost all modern systems ask for user identification (UID) and password before revealing that login was denied, even though the use of an invalid UID could have triggered an immediate refusal and the indication that the UID is invalid can save time and effort in many circumstances. This provisioning of false or misleading information benefits security at a small cost to normal users. Similarly, when looking for files in a system, protected directories and files appear not to exist rather than having their name, size, and other characteristics revealed. This concealment is widely considered a necessary deception for effective protection. There are many other built-in deceptions in modern systems that either cannot be disabled or are difficult to work without.

The use of deceptions that are built into existing systems is the default and it is widely used. While this is an acceptable approach, it is far less effective than options 3 or 4 at only a slightly lower cost. This is a reasonable option for companies with less than $10,000 of annual information technology budget because it bears no added costs and has some amount of protective effect.

The use of deceptions at firewalls is strongly advised for any company with information technology in excess of $10,000 per year. While the utility of firewalls is substantial in terms of limiting attacks, the utility is greatly enhanced when the firewalls do not reveal available attack paths to attackers. When a firewall does not use deceptions, most attacks rapidly focus on the legitimate paths through the firewall and seek out any weaknesses that may remain. For less than $10,000 an effective deception system can be placed at most interfaces to a firewall, configured for standard deceptions that do not interfere with the firewall, and allowed to operate effectively without harm to the network. This also provides rapid notification of many classes of attacks and in many ways is more effective at detection of attacks than standard intrusion detection systems.

The same principles that apply to external attacks apply to the deception of attackers who have broken into the company network and insiders who wish to do unauthorized exploration of internal networks. By placing deceptions at internal firewalls and routers, internal scans and attacks are greatly disrupted while intrusion attempts are rapidly identified. Again, the cost is on the order of less than $10,000 per firewall or router, and in volume the costs get considerably lower. This approach is strongly advised for any company with an information technology budget in excess of $100,000.

We advise against the use of deceptions within computers or the use of pure honey pot systems for small to medium sized businesses unless they are in the computer security business. This technology is not yet mature and it is expensive and complex to operate. Its primary use today is for research and not protection.

The key differentiating issue in the use of deceptions that are not built into systems and operational by default is their use in mitigating against event sequences with potentially serious negative consequences. In order to be effective, such defenses must conceal event sequences that attackers are likely to attempt to exploit and that have serious negative consequences. They can do this preventively by adding more event sequences that are likely to be tried by the attacker and that do not have serious negative consequences, thus increasing the search space of the attacker. Alternatively, they can be used responsively once an attack attempt has been detected to cover event sequences with potentially serious negative consequences from the attacker while permitting normal users and uses to continue uninterrupted.

Summary

Always use built-in deceptions. Augment deceptions with network-based deceptions if your total IT budget is in excess of $10,000 per year. If your total IT budget exceeds $100K per year, deceptions should also be used at internal firewalls and gateways.

Background checks: When should I do them?

Issue:

How much do employee background checks cost and how critical are they for my business?

Options:

Options are: (1) never do background checks on employees, (2) only check backgrounds on new employees, (3) only check backgrounds for key employees, (4) check all employee backgrounds.

Decision:

We recommend option 4 for all businesses. The cost is typically on the order of $100 per employee for a basic check and even if it is used only to verify the information on their application it is certainly prudent to know who you are hiring and that they have not lied on the application form. While many businesses select option 1 and never check employee backgrounds, the legal and brand reputation risk of not checking backgrounds can be severe, especially in the era of fear over terrorism. Option 2 may be prudent in some cases because of legal barriers against contractual changes for employees hired before a background check was required. Option 3 is a reasonable choice, particularly in businesses where many low-wage workers come and go but a few trusted employees remain over time.

Basis:

Criminal background checks are required for employees applying for certain jobs involving various kinds of trust, like school teachers and bus drivers. For employees doing sensitive government work, background checks are a required part of the security clearance process. Citizenship and work permit checks are also required for almost any legal job in the U.S. But many employers do the absolute minimum checking required; verification that a valid social security number was provided for tax purposes, and verification of a bank account for direct deposits of paychecks.

Option 1 is really a bad idea. In addition to potential legal problems, for most jobs some recommendation contacts and employment history are provided. Leaving these unchecked implies that you did not really need the information on the form and don't care about what they really did before, even if they were fired for criminal violations or harassment of other employees. If only for workplace safety, not doing a basic background check is a very risky approach

Option 2 may seem reasonable. After all, existing employees have been at the job for some time and are already trusted to some extent. Checking backgrounds on new employees can be part of a change in the employee contracts associated with changes in the business, while checking existing employees may create problems, especially if information gathered reveals something that could be seen as a basis for discrimination or retribution. As a result, option 2 has often been taken by existing businesses.

Option 3 is a basic cost saving measure. By limiting the number of checks to the most important employees, the costs are very low and the most critical people have been "checked out". Except for the problems associated with new hires, this might be a feasible approach and combining option 2 with option 3 may be sensible for a time.

Option 4 is preferred as a matter of due diligence. If a $100 check is not warranted for a new employee, the employee may not be worth hiring. The one exception is temporary, short term, or seasonal employees who come and go over short time frames and who do not have access to any critical assets. Migrant farm workers are good examples of employees for whom background checks would be infeasible and a poor business practice.

Summary

Background checks are low cost and highly effective at weeding out lies and criminality among potential workers. We strongly encourage checks whenever feasible and advise high quality more in-depth investigative approaches for cases when employees are being placed in positions of special trust.

Switches or hubs: Which should I use?

Issue:

Should I use switches or hubs in my internal infrastructure and what's the difference?

Options:

Options include (1) use hubs exclusively, (2) use switches exclusively, and (3) use switches in most places and have hubs sporadically based on cost limits for upgrades.

Decision:

We advise option 3. With rare exception, internal infrastructure will be more secure with switches than with hubs. While hubs are harder to defeat from a standpoint of denial of service attacks, switches will make the tasks of most attackers who have gained network access far harder and more complex. In addition, the changeover costs for companies with hubs may be substantial if undertaken as an independent effort rather than as part of periodic network upgrades.

Basis:

Hubs or switches are used to communicate between computers in most local area networks. Hubs copy all traffic to all ports, so that all systems share traffic on one virtual wire. Switches allow broadcast traffic to go to all ports but otherwise restrict traffic to only go to the port associated with its destination interface card (MAC) address. Hubs have historically been less expensive and made networks easier to debug. Switches are increasingly dominating the market however because making large and fast hubs is more expensive than making large fast switches. A factor of ten to one hundred increase in effective performance is also achieved by switches under many operating conditions.

Because hubs copy all traffic to all ports, anyone at a computer attached to any port within a company can potentially listen to all of the other traffic in their local area network. This is called sniffing. Sniffing tools are freely available for download from the Internet, and they include everything you need to decode traffic and look at it in full detail. This means that user identifications, passwords, files being transferred, exchanges between computers and servers or databases, email accounts, and email contents can all be easily observed. In many security assessments over many years we have found that this ultimately leads to unlimited access to most if not all resources within most networks. While sniffing traffic can be very handy at some locations for debugging, the dangers of allowing traffic sniffing usually far outweigh any advantages. For debugging, we usually advise that a few hubs be made available for network maintenance people so they can sniff traffic selectively from a small number of systems by temporarily rewiring a few connections. SPAN ports or similar mechanisms provide this sort of surveillance capability in switched systems.

One of the disadvantages of a switched infrastructure is that it can sometimes be attacked by insiders to deny service to others. This is because of poor design in some switches and inadequate control over others. The way switches determine where to send traffic is by examining the destination MAC address (the first 7 bytes of each packet of traffic) and comparing it to the last time it saw that same address as the source of traffic. The traffic is then directed toward the port that was last used by that MAC address. As long as all of the computers are used normally this works great. But attackers have tools that let them forge MAC addresses, and the result is that they can listen for broadcasts indicating the MAC addresses of other computers on the switch and then start sending packets as if they were from that MAC address, thus redirecting all traffic destined for those other computers toward the attacker. In high quality (more expensive) switches MAC addresses can be programmed in so that computers are only allowed to use the port they are assigned to, but most companies do not go this route. As a result, switches risk denial of service attacks from insiders.

Until recently switches were always more expensive than hubs, but this has changed lately because of the increased line speed needed to handle large numbers of ports at higher bandwidth. As a result, switches have started to dominate the fast switching arena and their cost has come to be less than hubs in most cases.

Summary

Switch your infrastructure. It's inexpensive, simple to do, has almost no effect on almost all normal operations, it is low cost, and it virtually eliminates one of the most common and simple attacks available to attackers today. If the cost is high for making a large-scale change, incrementally go to switches as you replace older equipment. Retain a small number of hubs for debugging purposes when you do conversions.

Penetration testing: What is it good for?

Issue:

Under what conditions should I use penetration testing to test network security?

Options:

(1) Never. (2) When there is an incident and it is desirable to detect the presence of similar vulnerabilities or residuals of the attack. (3) Periodically. (4) When systems are changed or installed. (5) During protection assessments.

Decision:

To the extent that penetration testing is undertaken, it should be directed at verifying the effectiveness (or lack thereof) of protection that is in place and be done as part of an overall protection assessment process. Option 1 is probably inappropriate, however, it does apply to systems with medium or high consequences in which tests should be run against the test systems rather than the live systems. Option 2 is appropriate as part of the detection and response process for incidents. Option 3 is reasonable for low-consequence systems, typically using inexpensive or free tools available over the Internet. Option 4 should be part of regression testing in the change control process. Option 5 is reasonable and appropriate if properly controlled and restricted to test systems.

Basis:

Many people think that penetration testing is a good way to either prove that they are secure or demonstrate to top management that increased vigilance is needed. But a penetration test can never demonstrate that you are secure. At best it can demonstrate that the testers failed to get in on this try. If penetrations are successful, this can be used to scare top management into supporting protection efforts, but this usually leads to temporary budget to fix the things found in the test and doesn't address the underlying causes of the protection failures, only the symptoms shown during the test.

The simplest and least expensive way to do a penetration test is to download tools like "nmap" and "nessus" from the Internet and run them against your systems. These are free packages that have graphical interfaces and do the same tests usually done by low-end professional penetration testers. The results are provided in relatively usable fashion along with pointers on how to mitigate the vulnerabilities they indicate. You can also buy pre-configured systems or services that run these tests for anywhere from $100 for a bootable CD-ROM system that does it to a few thousands of dollars per year to license a commercial product that repeatedly runs these tests against a network, either from inside the network or remotely from over the Internet.

If professional penetration testing is desired, it should always be done as part of an overall effort to enhance information protection. This is because the presence of vulnerabilities alone does not justify action. Risk comes from a combination of threats, vulnerabilities, and consequences. To meaningfully interpret the sorts of vulnerabilities detected in tests they must be put in the context of the threats that can exploit them and the consequences of their exploitation. As an integrated part of an overall assessment program, penetration testing can be a meaningful way to figure out where to best spend time and effort. Penetration testing can often be included in a protection posture assessment, or even a rapid protection assessment without additional cost, while penetration testing on its own by a professional will cost many thousands of dollars. Because tests cost money, only the least expensive tests are justified for low risk networks.

Top flight penetration testing is typically used when medium or high consequences and serious threats are associated with a system and when effective protection has been put in place by experts. The reason for this sort of test is to assure that the limitations of protections already in place are as they are believed to be. These sorts of tests are very expensive and only justified for very high valued targets.

Regression testing should be used as part of change control for all medium and high risk systems. This should explicitly cover all previously known vulnerabilities and no system should be permitted to operate at medium or high risk with known vulnerabilities present unless risk management has specifically decided to allow those vulnerabilities to be present and provided an appropriate reason. Testing should be done against the test systems used in change control and not against live medium and high risk systems.

A final note on penetration testing is in order. Every test of this sort has the potential to cause harm. Simple tests can sometimes crash computers and disrupt operations Mid-range tests under poorly controlled circumstances can have a similar effect and potentially leave residual vulnerabilities. Top flight tests often involve physical attacks combined with informational attacks and can produce serious consequences, sometimes even resulting in loss of life. The potential negative consequences of testing has to be kept in mind when making a prudent decision about doing these tests.

Summary

Penetration testing is a worthwhile activity if undertaken as part of an overall protection review, done by professionals and directed toward meaningful risk management objectives. It is also a simple way to test your own configurations at little or no cost. But it is not a panacea and should not be used on its own as a basis for making decisions about defenses.

Open or closed source: Which is better for me?

Issue:

Is open source software more or less secure than closed source, and should this impact my decision about which to use in which computers in my business?

Options:

Options include (1) only use closed source software, (2) only use open source software, (3) ignore this as an unimportant issue, or (4) use a mixed strategy.

Decision:

We advise option 3 or option 4. While there are many people taking positions on one side or another of this issue, we find that most of the positions are vacuous and self-serving. Option 3 is technically accurate, but option 4 is perhaps a more pragmatic viewpoint. Options 1 and 2 are both unrealistic.

Basis:

The fundamental security question surrounding open source and closed source is whether the value of having the source available and widely inspected is greater than the value of its concealment in terms of the resulting security. While there are theoretical arguments to be made on each side, the real question comes down to the quality of the software. Experience shows that high quality vendors produce more secure software and low quality vendors produce less secure software. In addition, a reasonable case can be made for having a more diverse software base if that diversity is applied so as to mitigate the risks associated with common mode failures - failures caused by the presence of the same fault in many copies.

Option 1 is infeasible because even the staunchest of the closed source vendors use open source within their products and because some elements of infrastructure are open source by nature. For example, the Kerberos infrastructure used for security in Microsoft products, a very staunch closed source advocate, is based on the open source Kerberos server written at MIT many years ago and relies on a common code base. In addition, there are free decompilers that can reliably and automatically convert most "closed source" programs into a usable source code form. So people who want to attack computers can get a good approximation of the source code for practical purposes if they want to anyway.

Option 2 is also unrealistic because there are many closed source software elements in almost computer system on the market today and because the lack of a freely available source does not make a product inherently insecure. For example, the basic input output system (BIOS) that forms the bootup process of most modern computers and the software that runs almost all disk drives are closed source.

Option 3, expresses the technical reality in that the quality of the software rather than the openness or closedness of its source code is ultimately the thing that leads to difficulty of attacks against it. Open source has the advantage of many eyes being able to view it and of being able to be rapidly altered by an expert defender to immediately mitigate against recently discovered vulnerabilities. Closed source has the advantage that it is somewhat harder to understand a decompiled version than the original source code and it takes a few extra hours to decompile and exploit it if you are a skilled attacker.

Option 4 is the most pragmatic approach to take. A mixed strategy involves selecting the right tools for the right jobs regardless of whether they are open or closed source. In cases where there is high consequence from failure and redundancy can be used to mitigate risks, use more than one solution so that any failures associated with a fault in one of the implementations is less likely to have commonalities with faults in the other implementations that result in similar failures.

Summary

Most of the open source / closed source debate has more to do with marketing than technical realities. Take a mixed strategy or simply ignore this issue and you will be better off than taking sides.

Security awareness: What should my plan be?

Issue:

What is a good security awareness program like for a business like mine?

Options:

Awareness programs come in many flavors, from scenario-based training and awareness to guest lectures, to light weight awareness programs. Typical options include (1) initial awareness training for all employees, (2) periodic security reminders, (3) guest lectures, (4) training sessions, (5) verified learning systems, (6) scenario-based policy awareness programs, and (7) booklets, pamphlets, and posters.

Decision:

For small businesses, initial awareness training, a quarterly newsletter or similar reminder, and training on how to use desktop computers is usually adequate for security awareness training. A good small business awareness program should cost only a few hundred dollars a year. For medium sized businesses, the same program with an additional monthly security reminder and email-based security alert should fulfill the need for most employees. Employees responsible for information protection should have additional security training on an ongoing basis. A really top flight awareness program should cost only a few tens of dollars per worker per year. Verified learning, scenario-based awareness, and guest lecturers are also good for medium sized businesses, but are often too expensive for small businesses. Large businesses should combine all of these elements in a comprehensive program integrated into other corporate training and awareness programs.

Basis:

Awareness of security issues is one of the best ways to get and keep employees involved in protecting the business. The use of security awareness programs can be viewed as a great benefit for employees if it is properly done. For example, many awareness programs help to protect employees from Internet-based scams and alert them to threats to their family from over the Internet. As a side benefit they also help the employees do a better job of protecting the assets of the company and keep moral high.

Small businesses with substantial risks associated with information systems need to have their employees on their side in order to effectively protect their information assets. There is never enough budget or expertise to do outstanding technical security for all of the systems and users, so one of the best hopes is that aware users will not do reckless things and will provide much of the normal vigilance needed for effective protection. Awareness of security rules and policies must be done at least once for each employee, typically as they start their new job. Otherwise they will not know what is expected of them. Ongoing awareness is necessary at least once per quarter because real-world events have shown that information security awareness wears off completely in less than 6 months. A quarterly newsletter, pamphlet, or a similar reminder often does this job well. One example is the "*porcelain press*", a security newsletter placed on the inside of bathroom stalls. Another is a review of interesting security issues that affect families and a security reminder for company security at a monthly staff meeting. Training on how to use desktop computers is also required when major changes are made, and this is another good place to include some security awareness. The total cost to the small business should only be a few tens of dollars per worker per year, and it's well worth the time and effort

For medium sized businesses, all of the things that apply to small businesses are true, except that there tend to be more incidents, more people, and more financial risk associated with information technology. For this reason an additional monthly security reminder and security alert system should be introduced. These sorts of reminders typically provide news-like articles of interest and reminders of elements of policy. Cartoons are sometimes used to keep it light. Medium sized businesses also tend to have considerable information technology operations and team members. Employees responsible for information protection should have additional security training on an ongoing basis. This sort of training is offered by the Computer Security Institute, and MIS Training Institute, SANS, and others. Those with security responsibility should also consider getting a CISSP certification.

Scenario-based awareness and training is excellent for hierarchically structured businesses, particularly when the scenario is used to generate or validate policy with top executives first. It takes about an hour per employee and two hours per manager and costs are on the order of $10,000 per year for all you need to do the customized training for your business. Guest lecturers are also good for medium sized businesses in cases where most employees can attend the lecture, either in person or via video link. Typical costs are in the $5000 per quarter range.

Large businesses should combine all of these in different parts of their business and provide management to assure that the program is efficient and effective.

Summary

Awareness programs are very effective and inexpensive and should be in place for any business that has significant risks associated with information technology.

Disaster recovery: How should I do planning?

Issue:

What disaster recovery plans should I have in place for my information technology?

Options:

Options include: (1) no disaster plan should be in place, (2) backup copies of critical data in a media safe (3) off-site copies of backups and a tested process for getting things going again, (4) a pre-arranged set of computer resources available for use in a short time frame, and (5) multiple sites with redundant operational capabilities.

Decision:

Each of these options is sensible under different circumstances involving information technology (IT) timeliness requirements and the relative criticality of IT to business operations. The matrix below describes strategies associated with different combinations:

Timeliness of IT	High consequence	Medium consequence	Low consequence
Seconds to hours	5	3, 4,5	1, 2, 3
Days to a week	3, 4	2, 3,4	1, 2, 3
Weeks to months	3	2, 3	1, 2

Basis:

The justification for a disaster recovery plan is that disasters happen all the time. Without a proper plan, a business may be unable to continue after the disaster. Insurance usually covers the physical losses to a business, but not the information losses or lost operating time, business, reputation, customers, and cash flow. Because information lends itself to being duplicated, it is a fairly easy matter to make usable backup copies of information and store them in locations that are unlikely to be affected by a disaster at the data's normal location. Similarly, most computer hardware can be replaced readily and on reasonably short notice if its replacement is planned in advance.

For businesses in which IT has low impact, an IT disaster recovery plan is purely optional. Most such businesses could simply operate without IT or replace the small amount of IT in place with a few new pieces of computer hardware and off-the-shelf software. If IT has a low impact that means that things like customer lists are not critical, accounts payable and receivable are not done in computers, and so forth. Options 2 and 3 provide for more rapid recovery of information technology and are advised if significant challenges or expenses would result from the loss of all IT capabilities and records. This is strictly a small investment in exchange for slightly reduced cost and increased convenience in case of a disaster.

For businesses in which there is a medium impact of information technology on operations, some sort of disaster recovery plan is strongly advised. If timeliness is important, for example, if product support requires computer access in order to answer questions that are asked 24x7 from customers in immediate need of help, outages can only be allowed to cause delays on rare occasions and for relatively short time periods. This means that, in a disaster, a rapid recovery process is needed, but it does not call for a secondary real-time backup site if the business impact of an IT failure isn't large enough to be worth the extra expense of a full-time redundant site. Business services will be down for hours to a day on rare occasions. In cases with less of a timeliness requirement, businesses can afford to be less prepared and spend less time, effort, and money on disaster recovery planning and preparation.

For businesses in which IT is high impact, the loss of IT capabilities is very expensive, perhaps life threatening, and could lead to business collapse. In these cases, disaster recovery must be done within required time frames, so higher surety and higher cost options are called for. If the IT is critical but time is not very important, the key is having a good set of backups that are well protected. This means that off-site copies of backups and a tested process for getting things going again in the required time frame for business continuity are necessary. In cases where only days to a week are available for recovery to normal operation, it may become questionable as to whether a proper set of hardware can be located and put in place at a reasonable cost in the necessary time. For that reason, depending on the hardware requirements, availability, and time, a pre-arranged set of computer resources may have to be available for use in a short time frame. For example, this is common in substantial insurance businesses, where instant availability is not critical, but confidence will be lost in a few days if service cannot be restored, and where systems typically in use are not available at any local office supply store. Option 5 is reserved for cases when time is of the essence. For example, banks cannot sustain outages of some systems for time frames on the order of hours without risking enormous losses. If a bank cannot clear transactions with the Federal Reserve system by the start of the next business day, they can lose enormous sums of money in interest alone.

Summary

The impact of IT and the criticality of IT recovery time on the business dictate the appropriate methods for IT disaster recovery. But surprisingly, business size does not matter, because the smaller the business, the less the cost of whatever methods apply.

Passwords: How often should we change them?

Issue:

What is a rational policy for requiring password changes for workers?

Options:

Options include (1) never change passwords, (2) change passwords when there is a specific reason to do so, (3) change passwords at convenient system changeover times, and (4) change passwords at regular intervals. Options 2-4 can be combined.

Decision:

We strongly recommend against option 1. We recommend Option 2. Option 3 is not a bad practice, but no obvious reduction in exposure is apparent. Option 4 is often called for in security standards and is reasonable in situations where user access is not well controlled.

Basis:

The basic reason to change a password is that the password in question may be known to an unauthorized user. The period of time between when an unauthorized user knows a password and when the password is changed represents a period of exposure to attack. The goal of password changes is to reduce this exposure. It is also important to consider that a fairly short exposure period can cause high consequences and, in many cases, within seconds to minutes of an initial break-in, "back doors" are put in place to allow reentry to the system even if the passwords are changed. For this reason, simply changing passwords may not be an effective action when an exposure is detected.

Option 1 is to never change passwords, and strictly speaking this is a poor approach. Never say never. In some cases changing passwords may not reduce exposures, but these cases are rare. For example, for a physically secured system without external user access and where only authorized users have physical access to the location with the computer, password changes may be of no value.

Option 2 is to change passwords whenever there is a specific reason to believe that there is an exposure. Clearly this is a sensible idea, but if carried to extremes may be too expensive for the level of the exposure. This approach calls for knowing when an event has occurred and what systems may be affected by it. Examples of events causing obvious exposures include the movement of an employee from one job to another, a known computer break-in, or a change in key personnel. In each case, access in excess of that necessary for the users' job functions are caused by their ability to access accounts using passwords. Figuring out which systems may be affected is somewhat complicated by interdependencies of systems and commonalities between systems. For example, if a file server password is exposed, it may affect all of the systems that use that file server. If the same user has access to multiple systems, they likely use the same or similar passwords on many of those systems and all of those systems are therefore exposed. There are many other similar examples.

Option 3 is to use convenient system changeover times as an event to trigger password changes. There is nothing inherently wrong with this practice, and indeed all new systems should have all user passwords initially set to non-default values. But this does not address the exposure issues and is thus of limited value.

Option 4 is recommended by most security standards and thus widely accepted as good practice. There are, however, some problems with changing passwords at regular intervals. Some of the major problems include; (a) People tend to have problems remembering the new passwords and write them down, which exposes the passwords further. (b) The only advantage to this is that it reduces the average exposure time by half of the password change rate. A 6 month password change time leaves an average of 3 months of exposure if a password is guessed or stolen. Since it only takes seconds to minutes to install a back door that makes the password no longer necessary, the advantages are not very great. (c) This is sometimes used as an alternative to removing user accounts from users who are no longer authorized to access systems, but it is far better to systematically remove those accounts and audit those removals than to depend on automated password change routines to do the job. (d) While many systems support the automation of these changes, some do not, so the management overhead may be substantial for enforcing this system.

Summary

Changing passwords is sometimes a very important step in securing systems, but setting a policy on password changes without considering the implications is often a waste of time and an inconvenience to users.

Remote access: How do I safely allow it?

Issue:

How do I safely allow access to company computers from employees at home and on the road?

Options:

Options include: (1) firewalls for remote computers, (2) virtual private networks (VPNs) or other encryption between remote and office systems, (3) dial-in access using telephones and modems, (4) firewalls that identify authorized remote use, or (5) don't allow remote access to internal systems.

Decision:

Option 3 is still viable and will likely remain so for quite some time. Options 1 and 2 are recommended for all businesses not using option 3. Option 4 is a poor approach today and is likely to lead to complex management overhead and unnecessary vulnerabilities. Option 5 is only viable for a relatively limited number of businesses today.

Basis:

According to most estimates, more than 50% of all workers work from home at least one day per week, and the numbers are increasing. Therefore, a secure solution for remote and home-based users is a necessity for many businesses. Most home-based users have Internet access, and Internet-based access to company computers is usually far more cost effective than dial-in access. Without encryption, traffic over the Internet is susceptible to surveillance and this method is commonly used to gain remote access to company networks by attackers. In addition, attacks against computers while they are in the user's home or on the road translate directly into attacks on internal networks when those users bring their computers into work.

Firewalls for remote user computers is a necessity if these computers are going to connect to the Internet. These personal firewalls cost less than $100 each and can be configured by the company to assure that the computers are reasonably well protected from obvious attacks. User training will also be required to assure that that they know how to answer any questions the firewall asks and what to do if they suspect something is not working properly. Internet connected computers should also have integrity or antivirus, antispyware, and anti-Trojan protection if they are running a Windows operating system.

Virtual private networks (VPNs) or other encryption between remote and office systems is also mandatory if Internet-based access is to be used. In addition to protecting sensitive data that may pass back and forth, this also protects against surveillance of user identification and password information that could be used to attack company computers and provides more comprehensive access to corporate systems using the same interfaces that are used within the corporate network. The cost is typically less than $100 per computer with a cost of a few thousand dollars for the central VPN server in most architectures. Some management is also required. But the cost is very low compared to the reduction in risk for almost any business.

Dial-in access using telephones and modems remains a viable alternative to Internet-based access. While the Internet seems to be less expensive in many cases, dial-in access is relatively inexpensive from most places. The security costs are far lower because most telephony is still more secure than Internet traffic, and if existing equipment and management systems are in place, the cost of transition to Internet may be more than the savings for some time to come. Care must also be taken to secure the dial-in point of presence against password guessing, directed attacks, and denial of service attacks. Voice over IP (VoIP) telephony is also dramatically reducing the security of voice communications while also dramatically reducing its cost.

Until a few years ago, firewalls that identified authorized home users without additional encryption were reasonably viable, but with rare exception, this is no longer an adequate approach. Internet addresses are almost all now dynamic, so address-based firewall protections are no longer viable. Authentication using one time passwords or other security tokens, while workable, doesn't deal with the encryption issues effectively. And maintenance of these connections is becoming more and more complex for businesses with more than a few employees. As a result, we recommend against this approach and recommend a transition to one of the alternatives indicated here.

For many businesses, remote use is not important, and in these cases, it should not be permitted. But the changing nature of information work generally makes this solution feasible only for very small businesses and very rare larger businesses. Still, if this can be done, it is the most secure solution.

Summary

A mixed strategy of effective firewalls and VPNs are the minimum recommendations for new remote access to business systems. Dial-in access continuation is recommended for existing dial-in approaches. Windows-based computers should also have additional integrity protection if they are being used outside of the corporate network. No remote computer that cannot defend itself should be allowed to access internal company systems.

Threats: How do I respond to computer extortion?

Issue:

What should a company do if someone attempts an Internet-based extortion?

Options:

Generally, the options include (1) pay the extortion amount, (2) call law enforcement, (3) call a security firm or private detective agency for emergency assistance, or (4) handle the technical issues internally. Options can often be combined.

Decision:

We advise against option 1, paying the extortionist. This almost always results in further extortion. We strongly advise options 2 and 3, calling law enforcement and calling for expert assistance, and against option 4, handling all technical issues internally, unless you have special expertise in this area. In all cases, internal security awareness programs should include corporate directions on how to react to an extortion attempt such as this.

Basis:

Extortionists are increasingly targeting office workers with deleted computer files, public release of internal information, or the installation of child pornography and a call to the police. They target anyone they can identify as a potential target, and assert and prove to some limited extent that they have access to the users' computer. They often start by asking for a relatively small amount, on the order of $20. If they get paid the price goes up and up. What can be done about this?

Some people choose to pay extortionists when the amount is small or the proof is good. The brand-related risk of being exposed in this way is high, but paying may ultimately result in a higher cost. If you choose to pay, be prepared to keep on paying.

The second option, and one that we always advise you to do in such cases, is to immediately inform local, state, federal, or other appropriate law enforcement. Make a police report, print and store paper copies of the extortion attempt, and follow a legal process. This option can be pursued in parallel with others.

A third option, and one that is often taken but rarely taken far enough, is to contact a competent Internet security and/or private investigations firm. These firms can be expensive in an emergency, but they are often worth it. They should start by determining the reality of the threat in terms of the technical reality of the break-in, mitigation strategies, and proper procedures for securing evidence. If they are not properly qualified for these sorts of activities, you should get another company that is. Doing these things poorly is often far worse than not doing them at all, because the extortionists sometimes decide to get nasty if they think they might get caught or if you are fighting back.

Some companies decide to take it on by themselves. Rather than pay an outside expert, they may have enough internal technical, legal, and other expertise to handle the situation. If you have the necessary expertise and extra time for your internal people to do this, it is an excellent solution.

One last caution is in order. In many of these cases, but certainly not all, an insider is involved in the extortion. Be very careful if you suspect an insider might be involved and contact law enforcement or other outside assistance privately, preferably not from your office or workplace.

Summary

It is becoming increasingly common to experience attempts at extortion based on Internet threats. The approach that is most often most effective is to contact law enforcement and outside experts to (1) determine the reality of the threat, (2) determine and implement appropriate countermeasures, and (3) if possible, catch the perpetrator.

Encryption: When should I transmit encrypted?

Issue:

When is encryption a good solution for securing my business information in transit?

Options:

Options are split into three dimensions. The first dimension is to (1) always, (2) when convenient and available, (3) when required by others, or (4) never use encryption. The second dimension is to use encryption for (A) sensitive information or (B) all information. The third dimension is using encryption (i) within internal infrastructure or (ii) when transiting untrusted networks.

Decision:

This decision is best represented in a matrix format with decisions associated with risk levels. For the purposes of this decision, risk levels are defined as:

- **low risk** when no known threats to the system or content apply and the consequences of information leaks are not important to the business.
- **medium risk** when there are known threat classes to the content or business but no specific threats and the consequences of information leaks are not life threatening or critical to business survival.
- **high risk** when there are known threat classes to the content or business and the consequences of information leaks are life threatening or critical to business survival, or when there are specific threats and the consequences to the business or content of information leaks are serious.

We recommend the following decisions:

Sensitivity	Location	Low Risk	Medium Risk	High Risk
all	internal	never	required	required
all	external	required	required	required
sensitive	internal	convenient	always	always
sensitive	external	required	always	always

Basis:

The use of encryption for information in transit, as opposed to other techniques, is specifically and solely for the purpose of preventing unauthorized revelation of content or information about the systems exchanging the content. It is expensive to do well and prevents internal surveillance that may be important to intrusion detection, network debugging, and other similar uses. Therefore, the only justification for encryption in transit comes from external requirements or risks.

In low risk situations: Never encrypt all content traveling through internal networks. It is expensive, unnecessary, and difficult to manage. If required for some contractual or other reason, external traffic should be encrypted. Sensitive information should be internally encrypted if it is convenient because while the risk is low, the cost is also low in this situation. External sensitive information should be encrypted if required for regulatory, public perception, or contractual reasons.

In medium risk situations, all internal network traffic should only be encrypted if required. Most information is not likely to be important if leaked, and this keeps unnecessary costs down without sacrificing anything critical. All external and internal sensitive information should be encrypted if it is convenient because, in the case of external information, it increases the difficulty of understanding which information is important, and for internal information, it doesn't hurt to encrypt if it is convenient. Sensitive information with value this high and identified threats should always be encrypted in transit, even internally.

In high risk situations, loss of life or similar high consequences may be the result of sensitive information leaks. As a result, all sensitive information should be encrypted in transit. Non-sensitive information should be encrypted internally if convenient and externally if required, for the same reasons as the medium risk situation.

Summary

Encryption of content in transit is a complex issue that involves considerable expense, and should therefore be applied judiciously. However, the use of low-cost encryption like secure socket layer (SSL) and similar methods for external connections to Web services is so inexpensive that it is always reasonable for use as long as it doesn't interfere with performance or network surveillance requirements.

Encryption: What should I store encrypted?

Issue:

What information should my business encrypt in storage?

Options:

Options typically include: (1) none, (2) sensitive, and (3) all information in (A) servers, (B) local user computers, (C) mobile user computers, (D) backup storage, and (E) critical high-value primary servers with strong physical security.

Decision:

This decision is best represented in a matrix format with decisions associated with risk levels. For the purposes of this decision, risk levels are defined as:

- **low risk** when no known threats to the system or content apply and the consequences of information leaks are not important to the business.
- **medium risk** when there are known threat classes to the content or business but no specific threats and the consequences of information leaks are not life threatening or critical to business survival.
- **high risk** when there are known threat classes to the content or business and the consequences of information leaks are life threatening or critical to business survival, or when there are specific threats and the consequences to the business or content of information leaks are serious.

We recommend the following decisions:

Location	Low Risk	Medium Risk	High Risk
servers	none	none	all
local	none	none	all
mobile	sensitive	sensitive	all
backup	none	none	all
primary	none	none	none

Basis:

The use of encryption for information in storage is specifically and solely for the purpose of preventing unauthorized revelation of content. It is moderately priced for entire file systems and media, but more expensive and harder to manage if only select content is to be encrypted. However, it is also far harder to do forensic analysis, data recovery, and management of systems in which content is encrypted. For that reason, encryption should be used only when required.

In low risk and medium risk situations: Never encrypt content unless it is being used remotely and in that case only encrypt sensitive information. It is often an option to only allow remote access to sensitive information stored on internal servers via encrypted communication to reduce the need to store sensitive information in encrypted form on remote systems. If backups are taken off site and stored elsewhere, encryption should be used in transit, however, be very cautious about encrypting backups because loss of keys or media errors can make the entire content permanently unusable.

In high risk situations: In high risk situations systems with sensitive data that could lead to severe consequences if released should be encrypted as part of full-disk or full media encryption on servers, local systems, remote systems, and backups. Remote systems should only be used if absolutely necessary for systems of this risk level. To the extent possible the systems with these requirements should be restricted to only computers and data absolutely necessary to run at these risk levels. When there is physical security present and when the data is a primary authoritative data source, the risk of loss of use may exceed the value of protection, so encryption is not recommended.

Summary

Encryption of content in storage is a complex issue that involves considerable expense and serious problems in recovery, and should therefore be applied only when necessary. The main utility is to protect against corruption or theft of stored data while in transit or when inadequate physical security is used.

Incident detection: How should I detect attacks?

Issue:

Should I use intrusion detection systems, and if so which kinds?

Options:

Options include: (1) ignore detection and wait till consequences reveal attacks, (2) occasionally or periodically examine log files and systems to detect intrusions, (3) use automation to collect and analyze log files and other indicators of intrusions, (4) use intrusion detection products that independently detect intrusions, (5) use a network-wide intrusion detection and analysis system, or (6) devise a system to detect event sequences with potentially serious negative consequences.

Decision:

The table below summarizes this decision.

Network size	Expertise	Low risk	Medium risk	High risk
small	low	1	3,4	6
small	high	2,3	2,3,4	6
big	low	3,4	Add expertise	Add expertise
big	high	3,4	4,5,6	6

Basis:

Intrusion detection mechanisms provide the means to detect unauthorized activities within systems and networks. The value of these systems is that they allow these unauthorized activities to be detected when they might otherwise not be detected, or to be detected more quickly than they would otherwise be detected. If the business consequences of these activities warrant the costs of intrusion detection, then intrusion detection is called for. Intrusion detection mechanisms range from audit records and methods to analyze those records, to automated systems that use surveillance methods to detect known intrusions or deviations from normal behavior. Essentially all such systems produce and unlimited number of false positives and false negatives, and investigation is required to follow-up on indications provided by these systems.

For any enterprise with a network involving hundreds or more computers (big), it is necessary to get additional expertise if existing expertise is inadequate. This can often be outsourced to specialist intrusion detection and response firms.

Ignoring intrusion detection and waiting till an attack is obvious from its consequences has two major problems. (a) Many attacks are not immediately detectable by their consequences, leading to far greater harm. (b) Attacks can happen quite quickly and covertly. In many cases the attack is over long before the consequences become apparent. The only exception is small low-risk networks.

Option 2 has the same problems as option 1 for the same sorts of attacks. But for other classes of attacks, like long term infestation of systems by intruders, it is marginally effective. Many attackers erase logging information about their attacks as part of their attack process, but this can be mitigated by the use of logging servers. We advise periodic checks with the period determined by the harm from different infestation times and random checks to augment periodic checks in case an attacker understands and tries to take advantage of the periodicity.

In option 3, automation is used to collect and analyze log files and other indicators of intrusions. This can provide more rapid detection, reducing the exposure time, and be automated, reducing the time and effort required to do the job. It produces false negatives, but so does human examination. It can also produce false positives, but the workload for investigation false positives is less than for examining the audit information by hand. For medium and high risk situations, internal automation is preferred. When there are a substantial number of available sources of information and they are not otherwise gathered together, commercial collection and fusion systems should be used and tailored to needs.

In cases where there are substantial vulnerabilities and consequences of undetected break-ins, intrusion detection products that independently detect intrusions are important. In cases without strong preventive controls, substantial consequences of unidentified attacks, and when there are intrusion types not detected by the normal control mechanisms, intrusion detection products that independently detect intrusions are advised. These mechanisms should be devised to detect otherwise unprotected event sequences that can lead to serious negative consequences and failures in other protective mechanisms.

Network-wide intrusion detection and analysis systems are typically used for networks with at least 100 computers. They consolidate audit and detection records, correlate them, rank them according to preset and customer modifiable settings, and present their results in real-time to network operations center staff. These systems are expensive but far less so than humans doing the same tasks.

Summary

Intrusion detection is advised for most companies with even moderate potential consequences from intrusions, but very different detection regimens are needed for different situations, and costs are substantial and must be weighed against benefits to make prudent decisions.

Incident response: Who you gonna call?

Issue:

Who should I call under what conditions to respond to attacks against my computers?

Options:

Options include: (1) do nothing, (2) use internal people only (3) call a private detective, (4) call a technical security firm, (5) call law enforcement.

Decision:

Option 1 is never appropriate - it only leads to more and more losses over time. Option 2 applies when (a) no crime has been committed, (b) no serious consequence can be averted by calling for outside help, and (c) internal expertise is adequate to the task. Option 2 is also often used until any of these things are known to be the case. Option 3 is appropriate when an investigation is called for and professional internal investigations staff is not available. Option 4 is used when in-house technical expertise is inadequate to the task or suspected of involvement. Option 5 is used when a crime has been committed. These options, other than option 1, can be combined or sequenced as appropriate.

Basis:

When under computer-related attack, the key business issue is to limit harmful consequences. Depending on the specifics of the situation, this is done in different ways and calls for different expertise. Depending on the circumstance, it may or may not be important to stop the attack soon, figure out who is doing it, act to protect against other actions by the perpetrator, repair damage, or continue operations. The necessity of these and other circumstantial conditions dictate the need for action, and the need action leads to the need for outside assistance in some cases.

The "do nothing" option essentially never applies. Even a computer system with no business value can be used to attack other computers, and this may result in liability to the company. Failure to act in the knowing presence of potentially serious negative consequences is the basis for gross negligence claims.

Most computer-related incident responses start with internal people undertaking investigations. Internal investigation is often needed to establish the potential for serious negative business consequences and to act to prevent further harm.

The one situation where internal investigations are to be avoided is when insiders are suspected of involvement. In such cases, private investigators are often called in, particularly those firms that are well known for carrying out investigations of computer-related crimes. These companies either have internal expertise or team with outsiders that have that expertise to facilitate all aspects of response. These sorts of investigations start out relatively low cost and grow in cost with the complexity of the case and the services required. Cost controls typically occur in intervals of a few thousands dollars beyond which further approval is required. Private detectives are often brought into cases with the assistance of the corporate attorney. Good recent examples of such cases include threats to employees via computer mail, sexual harassment of one employee by what appears to be another, and employees illicitly using company computers for starting their own business.

When inadequate technical expertise is available to solve the problems associated with attacks, outside expertise is the next step. For simple attacks, costs can sometimes be under $1000, but for the vast majority of such attacks, expect to pay anywhere from $5,000 to $25,000 before the technical issues are solved. In large scale incidents costs can escalate even further. It is very important to choose a technically competent vendor for this sort of work. When companies choose friends or acquaintances that do not have long experience in this field, the results can sometimes be disastrous.

When a crime has been committed or there is a threat to personal safety involved law enforcement is a viable aid. Failure to call law enforcement for certain types of matters may result in legal liabilities. For example, if a threat to health and safety is made via computers and it appears to be serious, private detectives may be the first call, but if such cases escalate, law enforcement is critical. If there is internal criminal activity, not calling law enforcement may turn decision makers into accessories after the fact and expose corporate officers to civil and criminal liability. For certain classes of crime, reporting to regulatory agencies may also be mandatory. For computer break-ins that involve an international nexus or involve financial crimes, the FBI may be the right call. As a rule. it is important to have thought through the possibilities in advance and to have a policy about when to call law enforcement. If this sort of decision has to be made in real time, errors can be very expensive.

Summary

There are a lot of resources available to help those in need, with costs varying over a wide range. The key to response decisions involving who to call is to have thought through the situation in advance. While the guidelines provided here are helpful in many situations, it is far better to have a personalized and well thought through plan.

Security costs: How much should it cost?

Issue:

What should the information protection budget be for a company like mine?

Options:

Common approaches are: (1) take a minimum-cost legal compliance approach, (2) take a comprehensive risk management approach, (3) decide to emphasize security as a key company priority, or (4) don't budget in advance for information protection, spend on a reactive basis when needs occur.

Decision:

Option 1 applies to situations in which information technology (IT) is a low priority in the business and in which substantial outages are not very important. In this case budgeted costs will be below 5% per year of annual IT budget but incidents will consume more resources and be disruptive. Option 2 will ultimately lead to optimization of spending and is advised for any business with a total IT budget or potential negative consequences of IT failure in excess of $100,000. For smaller companies, the cost of doing the risk management processes may exceed the value they bring. Typical budgets will be between 5% and 20% of total IT budgets. Option 3 is only appropriate as a response to a non-technical need, such as a reputation issue. In these cases budget may exceed 20% of IT budget. Option 4 is never advised and is usually a sign of a failure of management to think through the issues in advance. It may be reasonable in extremely small businesses. In some cases civil or criminal liability may result from this approach.

Basis:

Typically, systems and network administration and security costs should be on the order of 5-20% of the annual IT budget. It is hard to differentiate systems and network administration budget from security budget because it is usually the systems administrators who do the security implementation, and it is hard to differentiate the time spent on properly administering systems and networks from the time spent in securing them and responding to attacks. In the day-to-day activities of a good systems and network administrator, approximately half of their effort is security oriented, but it is common for days on end to be spent in reacting to an incident or implementing a new technical change, and these times are rarely accounted for properly.

Option 1 is a common plan. It involves doing only what is legally mandated and asking legal counsel how to minimally comply. Generally, this amounts to doing very little in advance of incidents, and having little budget and expertise in house in the computer security arena. This in turn leads to protection that tends to be ineffective. The budgeted costs might be in the range from 1% to 5% of total IT budget for this case, or on the order of a few cents per dollar of IT spending. For every $500 computer, only $5 or so per year would be spent on administration and security, not enough to even afford antivirus software on most PCs. Information technology has to be a pretty low priority for this to be the case, and of course incidents like a computer virus infestation will end up costing a lot more than they would if they were properly guarded against.

Option 2 takes the approach that management should balance spending with risks so as to optimize business performance. A systematic approach to risk management means understanding threats, vulnerabilities, and consequences and making decisions to avoid, transfer, reduce, or accept risks based on the business sensibility of the available options. Over time and experience, this leads to optimization of spending and utility. We advise this approach for any business with annual IT budgets in excess of $100,000. For smaller businesses, the cost of the risk management process itself starts to become so expensive that it dominates security costs. To put this in perspective, a business with this budget probably doesn't have even one full time person working in systems and network administration and likely has less than 20 total computer users. For companies that have used risk management effectively, systems administration and security costs tend to range from 5% to 20% of annual budget, depending on the specifics of the situation.

Option 3 tends to arise from one of two scenarios. One scenario is that a company sells security to others or is run by a security fanatic. In this case, the presence of more and better security is a matter of pride and proof that security can work. But even these companies must make sensible decisions eventually or go out of business. The other scenario is that a company is hit again and again or so hard that it starts to lose the faith of the market. In an effort to regain this faith, such a company might go to extremes in trying to achieve security, even at the expense of a great deal of inefficiency. In both cases this is an issue of reputation and brand, and not a technical decision.

Option 4 ultimately means that no actions are taken in advance for security. This means that regulatory violations are likely, company computers will be used to attack others, financial records and payables and receivables will be alterable, and so forth. Except in the smallest of businesses, this is certain to lead to big trouble. Computer viruses and worms will run rampant, company computers will be exploited by attackers against others, and credit card data and customer lists will be taken. Civil or criminal liability may also result from this approach.

Summary

Prudent information protection is fused with systems and network administration. Total costs of the combined activities ranges between 5% and 20% of IT budget.

Threats: Who would really try to attack me?

Issue

How do I assess the realistic threats to my company systems and how much do I really have to worry about information protection?

Options

Threat assessment is more of an art than a science. Options for threat assessment include; (1) ignore threat assessment and make guesses, (2) use the Web and other sources to search out information about real security incidents against companies like yours, (3) get a vendor to do a comparative study of similar companies, (4) get a high quality highly directed threat assessment done by an investigative professional, or (5) get a high quality general threat assessment done by threat assessment professionals.

Decision

Option 1 is not a good idea. For small companies that want to understand issues on their own and have weeks of effort to spend, option 2 is an opportunity to get a realistic understanding and it costs only time. Multiply the incident rate from your search by 20 for a realistic picture. Option 3 should be undertaken for a serious understanding of threats to any medium sized business and can be combined with a more complete assessment as part of the cost of the overall effort or undertaken on its own for a cost of less than $10,000. Option 4 is mandatory when a specific threat is known to exist and more details of that threat are important to know to take prudent safety precautions. Option 5 only applies to companies that have systems with high consequences of failure.

Basis

Threats are actors, people, groups, or nature, that can act to cause harm. Threats, vulnerabilities, and consequences combine to form risk. Risk can be accepted (which you do when you ignore it), transferred, avoided, or reduced. Without a clear understanding of the threat situation, making prudent decisions to accept, avoid, transfer, or reduce risk is pure guesswork. Companies that ignore threat assessment usually have too little or too much protection in the wrong places. Too little protection brings attacks. Too much brings excess costs.

Most companies take option 1 and ignore threat assessment. The guesses they make result in ineffective or excessive protection. But, if threat assessment costs a lot, the cost of threat assessment may exceed the increased consequences of under-protection and the increased costs of overprotection. Threat assessment is typically only cost effective for companies with substantial security budgets or loss potentials.

Option 2 is another popular option that has substantial benefits for properly skilled and trained searchers. However, most people aren't skilled at searching the Internet for threat information and evaluating what they read and most incidents are not published or reported to authorities. According to experts, less than 5 percent of all successful attacks that are detected are ever reported to the authorities. So searching the Internet for incidents is likely to produce a factor of 20 too few incidents to make a sound judgment. Knowing this and multiplying by a factor of 20 may help get a better handle on the real situation.

Option 3 is a sound decision for companies that have systems administration and security costs in excess of $100,000 per year or total information technology costs in excess of $1M per year. A vendor comparative study of similar companies typically costs under $10,000, but in many cases, a limited threat assessment is included in a rapid assessment or an information protection posture assessment, which are prudent for companies with these budget sizes.

Option 4 should always be taken in cases when a known threat has been detected causing substantial internal consequences or when the threat presents substantial potential for causing physical harm to individuals. For example, if an employee is threatened, an insider is suspected of computer abuse, or an extortion attempt is made against a company, a specific threat assessment is mandatory. The cost will be on the order of $2500 for a competent professional. The ultimate consultant costs from incidents such as these can be quite high, often in the range of $20,000 and sometimes reaching in excess of $100,000.

Option 5 is typically for companies with security costs in excess of $1M per year, when total information technology budgets are in excess of $10M per year, in cases when national security is involved, or in cases when international locations are involved in high risk areas of the world. For cases involving national security, government assistance is often provided in the form of threat briefings, but these tend to be a poor substitute for a professional threat assessment. Cost can range from $10,000 per year for access to global threat information from global threat analysis firms, to $25,000 for a directed threat assessment investigating threats to your company, to millions of dollars per year for government-funded investigations of specific threat groups as part of national intelligence.

Summary

Small companies should undertake minimal threat assessments unless they have a substantial information technology component. Medium sized companies and small companies with a substantial information technology component should have threat assessment included as part of their annual protection assessment efforts. If your information technology budget is in excess of $10M per year or a specific threat is identified with high consequences, you should get a professional threat assessment.

Backups: What should I back up and how often?

Issue

What information should I back up and how often should I do it?

Options

Options include; (1) never backup anything, (2) backup critical information when you feel concerned about losing it, (3) backup everything periodically, (4) create and maintain different backup processes and schedules for different information based on its criticality, or (5) continuously and automatically backup everything all the time.

Decision

For most businesses we strongly recommend option 3 or 4. Option 2 is a reasonable option to take, but should not be considered a replacement for option 3 or 4. Option 5 is too expensive and complex for most businesses, but in some cases it is applicable to specific systems because of regulatory or liability issues. Option 1 almost never applies.

Basis

Information is backed up because people and computers sometimes fail and information loss can cause business loss. Backups provide redundant copies of information so it can be restored if lost. For information that can be regenerated inexpensively, or for information that is incidental to the business, backups are only a convenience. But for information like orders, customer lists, accounts receivable and payable, telephone system number assignments to lines, and information that runs the business or facilities, backups are usually a necessity.

The option of never backing up anything is practically guaranteed to produce serious business losses in any business that depends on computers.

Option 2, backing up critical information when you feel concerned, is a reasonable thing for individuals to do, it does not represent a company approach to backups and has historically resulted in backup failures with substantial consequences. People sometimes forget to do backups, people sometimes backup files on the same systems as the originals are stored on, some people don't understand the importance of some information to the business, and many people just don't do backups because it is inconvenient. In case after case, disgruntled employees have deleted files and the backups for those files when they thought they would be fired or just before they quit. Because businesses do not adequately implement a company-wide backup solution, expensive forensic recovery processes or worse consequences occur all too often.

Option 3 is to implement a periodic full backup process that backs up everything available to the backup system on a regular basis. Whether this is done by a network administrator or an automated system, the backups should be verified on a regular basis by doing sample restorations. How often these backups should be done depends on technical factors like how much time and storage is required to do the full backup, and business factors like the cost associated with losing the information that was not backed up. We recommend that a more detailed analysis of this solution be undertaken by each company to determine the tradeoffs between costs and reduction in expected loss when failures occur in order to determine the proper backup period. This analysis should take no more than a few days of effort for most businesses. Systems to support backups of this sort over internal networks cost on the order of a few hundred dollars per computer, plus the costs of central backup servers, media, and other related operating costs. Backing up everything can also take a lot of space.

Option 4 is a more well defined and thoroughly thought out version of option 3. Instead of backing up everything with the same period, selection of what to backup and how often is done in a more detailed analysis. Many environments don't need full copies of all content, saving space and time by only baking up data. Others require only transactions be backed up. This approach requires that the business understand what information exists and what is important about it, that the location of information be identified, and that the system used to do backups allows the proper selection of what to backup and when.

Option 5 applies primarily to select systems within businesses where continuity of operation is vital or where loss of even a small amount of data can have substantial business consequences. For example, a bank needs to have a backup of every transaction that it accepts or a computer failure would cause loss of proper account balances. This is sometimes done by printing a paper record of each transaction at each point of presence, or it may involve real-time transmission to distant backup sites. Similarly, in manufacturing operations, permanent records of certain operations such as drug labeling and inspection records are required. In these cases, write once memories are often used to assure that the data cannot be erased once written. These systems involve special purpose solutions engineered to the specifications.

Summary

Backups are a necessity, and deciding what to backup and when to back it up is an important decision for most businesses. For most cases, periodic scheduled company-operated backups are prudent and should be undertaken. Improvements can be made for more cost effective and business efficient solutions if the systems and information are well enough understood. Special purpose backups for critical applications should be handled by independent engineering designs suited to the situation specifics.

Backup retention: How long should I keep them?

Issue

How long should I retain my backups?

Options

Options include; (1) retain backups forever, (2) retain different backups for different fixed periods, (3) retain backup data based on a business value assessment or (4) don't worry about retention periods.

Decision

Option 1 can be quite expensive and, while some backups should certainly be retained for an indefinite time, forever is too long. Option 2 is a common approach and is suitable to small to medium sized businesses that don't have the ability or desire to do more in-depth analysis. Option 3 is preferred and we support this approach for all businesses with substantial information technology departments. We strongly advise against option 4.

Basis

Backup retention periods should be based on the business value of the information in the backups, its availability for use, the capacity of the backup solution to retain data for long durations, and legal or regulatory retention requirements.

The only backup media known to last more than ten to twenty years are acid free paper stored in proper containment and etchings in metallic media or rocks. Etchings last longer if they are at larger granularity, which means that less data can be stored per unit cost for longer retention. Paper is a viable storage and retrieval media but it is heavy, expensive to create and maintain, sort through, and track. In practice, retention past seven to ten years requires that backups be restored and recreated periodically, and this results in substantial costs. Unless there is a critical need for long-term retention, indefinite storage is not advised.

Option 2 calls for differentiating different sorts of backups based on their retention time. The most common approach is to (a) Schedule incremental backups (where only changes are backed up) on a nightly basis and retain these for a month, reusing the same media on the same day each month. (b) Schedule full backups on a weekly basis, saving these for a month and reusing the weekly backups every month. (c) Retain monthly full backups for two years. (d) Use the last monthly backup of each year as the annual backup and retain it indefinitely. This scheme creates overlapping backups so that even if one fails others will be available with much of the same data.

Option 3 requires that a valuation of data relative to its retention value be made. This is strongly advised for any company with an information technology budget in excess of $100,000 and is often mandatory for any company that has regulatory compliance requirements. In this analysis, results should include retention time requirements as well as business value associated with retention or loss. Based on this assessment, backup retention requirements, data classification, and backup processes can be defined suited to the need. The cost of such an assessment is typically a few days of effort by a group of knowledgeable insiders. Option 3 also implies the need to consider data life cycle considerations, and this is critical for compliance with court orders and other similar legal and regulatory compliance matters. In option 3, data life cycle issues should be considered including duration of retention for normal legal purposes and tracking of data on backups so that court orders to retain data can be fulfilled in backup media as well as in primary systems.

Option 4 historically leads to backup failures and loss of business value. In some cases this results in business failure, while in other cases very expensive forensic processes result from inadequate backup retention.

Summary

Either a scheduled backup retention process for all data or a content-specific retention approach is advised. Backup retention should be intimately ties to data life cycle issues including timeliness of destruction and retention for legally mandated purposes.

Backups: How and where should I store them?

Issue

How should I assure that backups are effective even in case of a fire or disaster?

Options

Backup storage options include: (1) a closet or storage room, (2) the computer room, (3) a standard business safe, (4) a media fire safe, and (5) off-site storage.

Decision

We strongly advise the use of option 5 for long-term storage and option 4 for local short-term storage of backup media. Options 1, 2, and 3 are recipes for turning a fire or other disaster into a business collapse.

Basis

In order to be effective in a fire, flood, or other sort of disaster situation, backup copies of computer content must be kept safe, or they will be lost along with all of the business value contained in them. In order to assure safety, backups should be separate and different from originals, and the more separated and different, the better it is for assuring the ability to get back the information.

Options 1, 2, and 3 are simply ineffective and have turned small disasters into major business failures time and again. Storage in a closet, the computer room, or a standard business safe that is good for paper records will not be effective for electronic media. A fire that destroys the computers will almost certainly destroy the backup media and the storage closet if they are proximate. Standard business safes that protect paper from destruction reach internal temperatures that are high enough to cause computer media to lose its data. As a result, these three options are strongly discouraged for backup retention.

Option 4 offers effective protection of backup media while on site. Special computer media safes are available and designed to keep computer media safe for rated times at rated temperatures in case of fire. These safes are thicker, heavier, and more expensive than standard business safes but are a necessity for any backup that must survive a fire. Media safes for storing terabytes of data cost on the order of $1500 and can be ordered from FireKing or other similar vendors. Option 4 can be combined with option 5 for the combination of protections afforded.

Option 5 is strongly advised for all businesses for use in the long-term retention of backups. For example, weekly, monthly, quarterly or annual backups can be stored in a safe deposit box at a local bank for a few hundred dollars per year. This affords a high enough degree of security for most businesses and is quite cost effective. These backups will only be available for recovery on weekdays when the bank is opened. Other computer media backup facilities are provided for higher valued data through companies that ship media to remote storage facilities and provide shipment back upon request. This is a sound place to store backups for recovery from major natural disasters, war, and insurrection, however, even the best known storage facilities lose backups in transit. For example, Iron Mountain, one of the best known of these sites, lost 4 backup sets in the first quarter of 2005, including tapes with all of the data on 600,000 current and former employees and families of a major corporation. Encryption of backup media sent to or through uncontrolled locations is vital to their protection and verification of arrival in a timely fashion is required in order to assure availability. All other protection requirements associated with the data on backups must also be retained at off-site storage locations and inspection may be the only route to providing adequate assurance.

Summary

A computer media rated fire safe should be used for local backup storage, and a bank or other similar facility should be used for long-term off-site storage of backups.

Security consultants: When should I use one?

Issue

What are the circumstances under which information security consultants should be used and what should they cost?

Options

Options include: (1) Never bring in an information security consultant, (2) bring them in to provide expertise you don't have, (3) bring them in when you are short on available time to get the security tasks you need to do completed, (4) bring them in for an objective outside opinion, or (5) bring them in for political or personal expediency.

Decision

Option 1 is not a good idea for most small to medium sized companies because it usually implies excessive staffing. Options 2, 3, and 4 are all reasonable and should be undertaken as appropriate. Option 5 is almost never appropriate in information security.

Basis

There are three basic reasons that companies hire consultants of any sort; a lack of time, expertise, or perspective. While convenience is sometimes cited, this really translates into a combination of time and expertise. In some cases consultants are also hired for political reasons, such as hiring an executive's relative or a prestigious outside firm to review your books, but even this rarely flies without at least some degree of justification based on one of the three basic reasons.

Nobody knows everything there is to know about information protection, and on occasion, bad things happen that are too hard to manage with available staff, either because of time or expertise limits. It is a rare company that has no internal disputes, but some companies are good at handling these internally. Finally, almost any company can benefit from an outside opinion of their information protection posture. Otherwise, you lose perspective over time. For these reasons, option 1 is rarely a good choice except for very small companies with very little information technology dependence.

True security expertise is a rare commodity today. It usually takes at least 2 years of experience before security practitioners become reasonably well qualified at simple security tasks. For more skilled advisers, at least ten years of relevant experience seems necessary in order to gain in-depth understanding of the issues. To make good management decisions and also have outstanding technical knowledge is a true rarity. Unless your staff includes this sort of expertise in the area of interest, outside assistance may be the only way to address critical security concerns. The cost of such a consultant is on the order of $3000 per day or more. Some charge up to $8000 per day, but just charging a lot doesn't make you a real expert.

When you are short on available time and have many specific tasks to do, second tier security consultants will often be adequate, under proper guidance. Most security consulting firms have these sorts of people available to do work for costs ranging from $75 to $150 per hour. An appropriate supervisory level person to manage them will typically run anywhere from $150 per hour to $250 per hour. These are generally different people than the people brought in when expertise is the critical factor in the decision.

For objective outside opinions, it is almost always important to have true experts. In these cases, some companies make the mistake of hiring the expert for internal political purposes of validating one or another point of view. Any expert worth having in will not bend to political pressures and will give a straight answer. These are the same experts that are typically used for option 2.

It is rare to hear companies use the name of their security consultant as part of their marketing. Calling in an executive's relative is almost universally a poor idea for at least two reasons. (1) There are very few experts in security and mistakes in this arena can be very costly. Unless the individual is a top-flight expert with a long and spotless history, it is a mistake to call them in for this purpose. Call them in for some other consulting effort. (2) The second reason not to bring in a close friend or relative is that they are not independent, and independence is very important in an information security consultant. If the ideas or results are biased by friendship, they are likely to not be the best security decisions. There are also far more historic incidents where relatives collude to the detriment of stakeholders than non-relatives. No top-flight expert with a long and spotless history will enter into such an engagement with a large business without prior disclosure of the relationship and proper acceptance and management of the process by independent parties within the organization.

Summary

Security consultants are normally brought in for lack of time or expertise, or objectivity. They cost on the order of $2000 per day when they are providing primarily time, and typically cost more than $3000 a day when they are used for expertise or objectivity.

Security policy: How much do I need?

Issue

Do I really need information security policies at all, and if so, which ones do I really need?

Options

Options include: (1) no security policies at all, (2) acceptable use policies, (3) legal and regulatory related policies, (4) a wide array of standards-based and other policies.

Decision

For most small businesses, no policy is legally required, so option 1 is viable but not advised. Option 2 is a common selection and it is advised for those not covered by specific regulatory requirements. Option 3 is necessary if mandated and should be in place under these conditions. Option 4 is really a big company policy or a policy for companies with a lot of intellectual property issues.

Basis

Policies form the basis upon which governance operates. The governance issues in very small businesses tend to be minimal because everyone knows everyone else and what they are doing. But as businesses grow in size, increasing amounts of governance are required. But even the largest company may properly only have minimal information security policies for most employees if there is little in the way of intellectual property being protected. Generally, governance is best when it governs least. Only put in place policies you need.

Policy free environments are the nicest ones to live in, until someone does something they aren't supposed to. When they do, the presence of an acceptable use policy can be the difference between legal liability and none, between termination for cause and retention of an employee you would rather not have, and between successful protection of your business and its loss.

An acceptable use policy is adequate for information protection issues for most small to medium sized businesses. Typically these policies include but are not limited to: (1) declaration that this is a Federal Interest Computer system and network, (2) that it is for authorized use only, (3) that there is no expectation of privacy, (4) that no solicitation is permitted, (5) that testing of security is only permitted by those authorized to do so, and (6) that response can and will range from nothing to termination to legal action at the sole discretion of management. Additional policies are required surrounding HR, legal issues, and all other aspects of employment, but they are not information protection specific.

Regulatory compliance mandates some policies, including a policy that states that all regulatory and legal requirements will be fulfilled. Regulations like the Health Insurance Portability and Accountability Act (HIPAA), the Sarbanes Oxley Act (SOX), the Gramm-Leech-Bliley Act (GLBA), and others require that notice of various kinds be provided and that specific policies about separation of different kinds of data, data retention, and nondisclosure be in place. The specifics are called out in each regulatory scheme and each should be followed to the letter of the law whenever possible in order to assure that negligence is not chargeable.

Big-time information security policies are for companies with a lot of intellectual property or high information technology related consequences. These companies often have anywhere from 40 to 400 policies, sometimes have different and inconsistent policies for different divisions, and often do not track those policies and their proliferation in a meaningful way. They produce policy in response to situations without integrating those polices with other policies and rarely update existing policies over time. This situation ultimately leads to large policy holes where different policies refer to each other for policy elements that don't actually exist anywhere. They often have inconsistent coverage of the same policy issue in many places because they are not tracking to standards and they are writing policies that cover specific sorts of systems rather than creating broad policies and using control standards to specify policy implementation in specific systems.

For these situations, it is best to do a comprehensive policy reconciliation and rewrite. Proper reconciliation can be done for as little as $2500 per existing policy and produces a policy map that brings clarity to the existing policies and their coverage. From there, a by-reference policy rewrite mapping existing policies into a selected standard typically takes a week or two of effort and a rewrite of policy from the by-reference policy takes another week. The result is typically a new comprehensive and consistent policy that retains all of the existing policy elements but is simpler and more easily understood and tracked. The elements of policy that rightly belonged in control standards are left for ongoing use at the next level of detail.

Summary

Governance is best that governs least. Keep policies to a minimum, only invoking those you really need for the circumstance. If your organization is very large and complex and hasn't properly tracked policies, you should consider a comprehensive policy reconciliation and rewrite.

Network zones: How should I zone my network?

Issue

Should I separate parts of my internal network and how should I decide how to separate them?

Options

Options include: (1) no zone separation, (2) several zones for different business functions, (3) many small zones for individual projects, (4) a small number of zones with subzones for risk disaggregation.

Decision

For most small businesses, a single internal network zone is used with an optional demilitarized zone (DMZ) or external service provider for servers accessible from the Internet - option 1 is viable. Option 2 is a common selection for medium sized businesses and is advised for most businesses until they become large and complex. Option 3 is hard to manage and only really appropriate for large businesses that consist of many smaller almost independent businesses. Option 4 is the large enterprise solution of choice.

Basis

Most small businesses have relatively few computer systems and they all work together to facilitate the same effort. Separation takes time, effort, and expertise. Little physical separation is typically in place, little expertise is available, and the cost is substantial, so at best there may be an Internet network address translation firewall in most small businesses. The computer-related issues are typically not so great that adequate backups and restoration times of days are not devastating to the business, so the costs do not justify the benefits for complex network separation.

Several zones for different business functions typify medium sized businesses. They may have a manufacturing function, a financial function, a sales and marketing department, an HR department, and several other similar areas, each with its own user base and little common functionality crossing these boundaries. In this case, each department can have its own local area network (LAN) that run more or less on its own. There is typically enough information technology expertise to allow for at least one full time employee dealing with networking issues and that employee can easily deploy a small number of internal network segments using VLAN technology, firewalls, or switch configurations to make the networks relatively independent of each other. This will also limit the spread of viruses and reduce the debugging effort when network problems occur.

As the number of zones increase, the management complexity also increases, especially for enterprises that grow to larger sizes. Sheer numbers make departmental separation as the sole means of protection hard to do. The need for internal applications to more highly integrate drives less separation between departments and even more complexity in dealing with the interactions. The management complexity also goes beyond what can be handled by a single individual, necessitating more group efforts and more unified and standardized approaches. At some point the transition has to be made to the large enterprise model.

The typical large enterprise will have several zones of increasing business import including perhaps:

- an Internet zone that is untrusted,
- a demilitarized zone (DMZ) for front-end servers that face the Internet,
- a business zone where most workers work most of the time,
- an application and server zone that has back-end application servers,
- and perhaps a high risk zone where large databases and their contents lie along with business critical systems and high consequence systems.

In addition, there may be:

- an audit zone used to retain audit records produced throughout the enterprise and
- a control zone to control the network and manage its critical functions.

Within these zones, which are typically separated by high complexity and heavily managed firewalls, reside subzones that are used for additional separation to limit the aggregation of risk, to group like with like, and to prevent outages or packet floods from interfering with other business functions.

Summary

Network zoning is dictated largely by business size with small businesses having few if any zones, medium businesses having zones partitioned by business function, and large enterprises having zones based on risk profiles and subzones for risk disaggregation.

Network zones: What should I put where?

Issue

Given my zoning strategy, what systems, data, and people should I put in which zone?

Options

Options include: (1) put systems with like data together and people with like jobs together, (2) put systems with similar risk profiles together and people who have to use those systems together, (3) put Internet-accessible systems in a DMZ, most systems used every day by direct user contact in a business zone, back-end machines in a more restricted zone, highly sensitive or critical data in a more restricted zone, network control systems in a control zone, and audit trails in an audit zone, and (4) limit zone content based on management specified risk management thresholds associated with the protective measures in use.

Decision

Option 3 is good for large enterprises as a first-level approach but may be too complex for smaller businesses to manage and is only a representative of a larger set of strategic possibilities. Option 2 is also sensible in that it allows the security measures designed to protect properties of a particular sort to be applied uniformly to similar sorts of content. It is advised as an efficient approach to partitioning but it must be balanced with option 4, which should apply to all enterprises regardless of size. Option 1 is only viable as a first level strategy for small to medium sized businesses because it is too simplistic to meet large enterprise needs, but it is viable as a second level strategy within zones for all enterprises.

Basis

Putting people and data with similar people and data implies that all people with similar jobs and data with similar characteristics require the same level of protection. This is probably a poor assumption for two reasons. The first reason is rather obvious, the same data is used by different people for different purposes, and some of those purposes are far mare critical to the business than others. The second reason is that it defies the notion of separation of duties. Audit information, control information, and submit and commit cycles associated with high valued operations should all be separated, and that is the purpose of zones. Putting like with like within partitions that provide separation is feasible, convenient, and commonly done.

Putting systems with similar risk profiles together is sensible because the risk profile is what should be driving the protection profile. As a matter of efficiency, it is easier to put one instance of a protective measure in place than multiple instances of the same barrier. But this is problematic because (1) similar risk profiles do not mean identical configurations of protective mechanisms, and (2) as risk levels increase separation becomes required for disaggregation. The former problem is very damaging in this approach since the very limits placed on protocols for one application may have to be violated for another. Integrity may be critical for one application while availability is more important to another. Thus risk level alone cannot be used as a basis for separation. However, similar risk level should lead to similar surety requirements on protective measures.

Risks should be disaggregated above some threshold in every enterprise. Whether it is keeping a backup copy of critical financial data for a small business or requiring separation of duties for large financial transactions for a large enterprise, it is necessary for management to make a determination of how much risk they are willing to group together under common failure modes and what scenarios they are willing to allow to destroy the entire business or what portion of it.

The structure commonly identified in generic terms for large enterprise zoning is based on business sensitivity with increasing numbers of better barriers between increasingly sensitive content and large and larger volumes of content. In addition, parallel separation of control and audit is used. The particular structure and placement identified here, or a variation on it, is often in large enterprises as a first level approach to placement because it simplifies management by consolidating requirements and mechanisms. While it sacrifices some surety it does so at substantial cost savings over a component-at-a-time approach. Within this structure, additional structure of the sorts described by the other options is important and should be implemented.

Summary

All of the identified strategies apply to placement but in different proportion for different sizes and types of situations. Some structured approach should be taken in almost all cases and the placement is tightly linked to the zoning approach, so these sets of decisions should be made together.

Data center redundancy: How many do I need?

Issue

I understand that I need redundancy to protect business continuity and provide for disaster recovery, but how much redundancy do I really need?

Options

Options include: (1) a single data center well protected from all identified threats, (2) two data centers, a primary and a backup, or (3) more than two data centers distributed across the regions where the business functions.

Decision

For most small businesses, a single data center, if there is a data center at all, is reasonable and prudent, so option 1 is a good choice. For a medium sized business with only one facility where all value of the enterprise resides. Option 1 is also viable because any event large enough to cause serious damage to the data center if it is well protected within the facility is likely to also impact all of the other elements of the business. Option 2 is good for distributed medium sized businesses or large enterprises that don't have a high threat profile, are not highly dependent on information technology, and are not highly geographically diverse. Option 3 is appropriate for any large enterprise that is geographically distributed or a medium sized business with high dependence on information technology and geographic diversity.

Basis

For small businesses, the cost of redundant data centers is fairly high and there is rarely data so critical to operations that multiple data centers are justified. A better strategy is often to have backups retained off-site, perhaps in a bank safe deposit box or fireproof media rated safe. If and when disaster strikes, the backups can be used for recovery without high losses to the business. The cost is low, the consequences are relatively low, and the resources are spent if and when recovery is needed. Of course the backup and recovery process must be tested periodically to assure that it will in fact function. Similarly, a well protected data center inside a single facility medium-sized business is adequate because there is no reason to protect the data center more than the rest of the business it depends on.

For medium scale businesses that are geographically diverse or highly dependent on information technology and large enterprises that are not geographically diverse, a primary and secondary data center are appropriate in order to assure continuity of operations across facility-related failures without long delays in recovery. Backups are mandatory, but these backups should be reflected in a timely fashion in the backup facility so that recovery and continuity of operations is assured at all times and within time frames that prevent serious negative consequences to the information utility of the company. The backup site should also be populated with adequate personnel to continue operations if the primary fails catastrophically and people cannot be transported to it. Putting all of the enterprise eggs in one basked or allowing single points of failure is irresponsible.

For any large enterprise that is geographically distributed or medium scale enterprise with high dependency in information technology and geographic distribution, geographically distributed data centers in major regions of operation should be in place to support critical business functions while also affording higher performance for the local area and retaining appropriate expertise in multiple facilities to continue business operations even if regional disasters or government failures take place. The larger and more distributed the company, the more opportunities there are for geographic distribution and redundancy. Not all data centers must have copies of all content. Rather, distribution of content over data centers and levels of redundancy should be determined by utility of local versions of information combined with business impacts of failures. As in the two data center case, recovery times are important to understanding the design of the redundancy. Infrastructure, and other dependencies should be considered, and personnel redundancy is critical.

In all cases, backups facilities, backups, and backup and recovery processes should be tested and verified periodically. This is typically done at least once per year as part of business continuity planning efforts. Backups should be verified as they are taken, so that loss of backup data because of media failures should never be at issue for the short run. Redundancy is a complex subject and the exact number of redundant data centers is highly dependent on the criticality of information. Many financial institutions have five or more data centers each capable of running all financial transactions. Many companies are sufficiently diverse that they have limited redundancy for individual systems, but many facilities with data centers holding different capabilities, so that only a small fraction of the business fails if a data center is lost. Less diverse businesses and businesses undergoing data center consolidation for cost savings sometimes end up with inadequate redundancy. Some large enterprises have had complete business failure because of a single point of failure in a business critical system.

Summary

Redundant data centers are requited in all but small business and single facility businesses. The level of redundancy is driven by size of the enterprise and criticality of the utility of information technology to business function.

Backup facility distance: How far should I go?

Issue

How far away do I have to put redundant data centers and people to assure reasonable business continuity?

Options

Options include: (1) no distance requirement, (2) at least 5 miles away, (3) in another city, (4) at least 250 miles away, and (5) on another continent.

Decision

For enterprises with no requirement for a separate backup facility, Option 1 is fine. Option 2 is used for highly localized enterprises in wishing to only protect against facility failures, riots, explosions, calamities on local highways, and similar conditions. Option 3 is used for regional enterprises not trying to continue operations in the face of large-scale events like hurricanes. Option 4 is appropriate for any large enterprise not limited to a region and is suitable for most natural disasters and most single event human activities. Option 5 is for multinationals that are global in nature and need to survive national level governmental changes, severed international communications, and wars and insurrections. Options 4 and 5 are also helpful in assuring high performance because global communications takes time and tends to be less reliable than local communications.

Basis

Distance requirements for backup facilities are driven entirely by scenarios that can lead to simultaneous loss. These in turn are threat driven. If an enterprise has to be able to survive limited nuclear attack, government insurrections, regional and world wars, and comet strikes that don't end all human life, transcontinental diversity is a necessity. There are many global multinationals that have this requirement and the efficiency gained by reducing this sort of redundancy does not justify the collapse of the business under conditions that, in the case of wars and governmental changes, happen quite frequently.

Many enterprises operate within only one continent or country, or substantially do so in terms of their need for information technologies associated with business continuity. In these cases, distance becomes an issue when regional events take place. In the US, for example, there are hurricanes that effect one region, earthquakes in another region, floods and storms in another region, winter related infrastructure failures in another region, and so forth. If the enterprise exists only within a certain region, then it doesn't particularly help to have redundant data centers elsewhere because they will be of little use when the rest of the business does not operate. The exception is the large enterprise that is dominant in a region but has enough diversity in operations to continue even when that region is hit by a regional event. Enterprises that cross regions usually have substantial facilities in more than one region, and these are often, but not always, ideal locations for redundant data centers.

In some cases these data centers may not be completely redundant but rather may have a primary function and a backup and recovery capability. Another common approach is to use one location for research and development and the other for operations. Since the same sorts of systems are used in each and separation of duties are required for medium and high risk elements of information technology operations, it is relatively low cost to physically separate the functions, use redundant hardware in the facilities, and use the redundant operational expertise of research, development, and testing in one location for operations if the primary operational center fails. If the secondary fails, research and development may collapse but operations continue.

For strictly regional companies, city to city redundancy is called for unless the enterprise is single facility or very limited in geographical scope. By spreading across cities, local government failures, telecommunications outages, common energy and infrastructure failures, most riots and fires, many tornadoes, hurricanes, earth movements, most floods, and many other similar failure modes can be avoided, Care must be taken to assure that commonalities are avoided in each of the interdependent areas so that business continuity is assured. Cost differences are typically very small for assuring proper infrastructure redundancy, but expertise is needed to verify this redundancy.

For very small localized businesses, if the owner survives, a set of backups that can be recovered within days to weeks and the ability to purchase new hardware is adequate, so redundant data centers are not a requirement at all. To the extent that there is redundancy, most protection is against single facility failures such as the main place of business burning down or some service outage. Redundancy may be limited to a backup tape taken home with the owner at night or every week.

Summary

Distance requirements stem from the causes of failure that the enterprise wishes to or has to survive. The larger and more diverse the enterprise, the larger the distances should be.

Detection and response: How fast should I be?

Issue

How quickly do I have to detect and respond to incidents?

Options

Options include: (1) as fast as possible, (2) as slow as I can be without causing a great deal of harm, (3) detect things that have obvious impacts and respond to them based on available resources and business impact, (4) detect and respond in time to mitigate potentially serious negative consequences.

Decision

Option 4 is the best solution in terms of meeting the enterprise need, but it is harder to do than the other options and requires considerable thought, planning, and expertise, and it should be used only in medium and high risk situations. Option 3 is commonly used in many companies and it works for obvious large-scale events, but it is very bad at dealing with subtle attacks and incidents tend to spin out of hand. It should be used for low consequence situations. Option 2 is good to minimize costs of response, but it often leads to inadequate detection and poor response, and without adequate analysis in advance, consequences may be higher than you think. It is feasible for small and smaller medium sized businesses. Option 1 takes a lot of resources that might be better applied elsewhere. It applies only to high risk environments where costs of defense are outweighed by consequences of failures. A mix of Options 1, 3, and 4 for high, medium, and low risk situations is reasonable in many cases.

Basis

Option 1 is very expensive and implies an eternal and unlimited amount of effort. Eventually budget limits the rate of detection and response, but the optimal point is usually far earlier. Simulations have shown that for incidents producing very rapid consequences, this works well, but many incidents are not this way and excessive speed of response carries high costs. The maximum speed approach also leads to errors and sometimes causes worse problems in the response than the incident would have produced on its own. It should only be applied to situations in which the consequences are very high and a well-defined process can be created that assures failures are in safe modes.

Option 2 is hard to do well. While going slowly has advantages in terms of costs, it has the major disadvantage that large losses can happen quickly. Slow response can turn minor incidents into catastrophic failures. Large businesses have failed in one-time incidents that required rapid reaction but got only a slow reaction. While delays may work for some decisions, this is not one of them.

Option 3 tends to produce results that end up being too late. In addition, they tend to be rather embarrassing to those tasked with security who are supposed to know about problems before the users do and mitigate them before business impacts become obvious. By the time business impact is analyzed, it may be too late to mitigate consequences. For that reason, this regimen should only be used to manage low risk situations in which the business consequence is known to be relatively small. In that case, this approach is cost effective and reasonably efficient as long as the total incident levels can be kept to within reasonable rates.

Option 4 would be perfect if it weren't so hard to do. In order to mitigate event sequences with potentially serious negative consequences through timely detection and response, you must first understand the event sequences and their consequences. This analysis is beyond the apparent capacity of most enterprises today, presumably because the risk management process does not adequately explore the nature of risks. Without a clear understanding of business risk, this is problematic. Fortunately, the requirements of Sarbanes Oxley regulations mandate that enterprises start taking risk management more seriously in order to present realistic risk information to potential and current shareholders. If this process is used wisely, it should greatly facilitate the internal decisions about what event sequences are of such consequence as to warrant timely detection and response. From there the time frames required for risk mitigation and the resulting techniques to be applied should become apparent. Because of the time and effort required for this level of understanding and design, it is appropriate only to situations in which adequate consequences are present to justify the cost of being careful in the defense. Thus its applicability for medium and high risk situations.

Realistically, a mix of option 3 and 4 are most commonly appropriate, and some enterprises may choose option 1 for high risk, option 4 for medium risk, and option 3 for low risk.

Summary

A differentiated approach to detection and response should be taken that associates different regimens with different situations.

Risk aggregation: How do I control it?

Issue

How do I identify and control the aggregation of risks associated with information technology?

Options

Options include: (1) do ad-hoc risk aggregation mitigation when designers happen to notice the issue or when events drive you to it, (2) analyze aggregated risk for systems that have obvious business criticality, (3) do a periodic risk aggregation analysis and mitigate problems on a scheduled basis, (4) fully integrate risk aggregation into operations and change management practices.

Decision

For most small businesses risk aggregation is so commonplace that it is only mitigated when there is a failure that requires a repair. Thus option 1 is used. Option 2 is acceptable for medium sized businesses who are not using multiple data centers. Option 3 is good for enterprises that don't have a strong change management system in place. Option 4 is preferred for all large enterprises and medium sized businesses with multiple data centers.

Basis

Option 1 is often used by enterprises of all sizes, but risk aggregation is a serious problem and the root cause of many large losses and some business collapses. For that reason, except for small businesses and medium sized highly localized businesses that don't justify redundant data centers to mitigate highly localized risks associated with a single facility failure, this should not be used as the approach. It is simply too dangerous and ad hoc and systematic approaches are called for when risks are nontrivial.

Option 2 begs the question of what is obvious and to whom. A good quote comes from Virgil Gligor who, when discussing a computer security-related issue said:

> *"If you think about it intensely for three years, it's obvious"*

Things in information protection are complex and only become obvious once you have studied then for a long time. An alternative is to get more systematic and use checklists or similar tools that cover the issues, like those provided in the CISO ToolKit's Security Checklists, Governance Guidebook, and Security Metrics series or the items listed in standards. This is closer to the approach used in option 3.

Option 3 should be used in any enterprise that is large enough to warrant redundancy and in which a systematic change control process is not in place. If a strong and systematic change control process is used, then it will also include this coverage. Periodic review is appropriate through the audit process, but unnecessary from a security execution perspective because it is already covered in real-time by the change management process.

Option 4 is preferred for medium and high risk environments that should be under strong change controls and thus should deal with risk aggregation issues effectively as part of their normal protection processes.

Risk aggregation defenses are really the reason that redundancy is used, but some issues, like backups and multiple data centers are more obvious than other risk aggregation issues like localization and employee dependencies. A full scale risk aggregation analysis is reasonable and prudent for medium sized businesses and mandatory for large enterprises and public companies.

Risk aggregation should generally consider all of the interdependencies of business utility. This includes but is not limited to; people, programs, data, libraries, files, input and output, operating systems, configurations, domain name services, identity management services, back end processing and storage, protocols, platforms, networks, wires, routing, access, power, cooling, heating, air, communications, government, environment, supplies, safety, health, and facilities. Each of these aggregate risks due to multiple uses and all of those uses have to be summed in order to understand the risks associated with integrity, availability, confidentiality, use control, and accountability and the lack thereof that may result from any identifiable failure modes.

Summary

Medium and large enterprises and all public companies should do risk aggregation analysis at least annually, and if change management systems are in place, they should integrate risk aggregation issues.

Change management: How should I handle it?

Issue

How do I manage changes to information technology?

Options

Options include: (1) just let change happen and keep backups in case you have to revert to them, (2) create a system to identify and track changes larger than a particular management-defined consequence level (3) apply sound change controls.

Decision

For most small businesses, option 1 is used, and this is reasonable except for particularly high tech or software industry small businesses. Option 2 is a good solution for medium sized businesses but without some systematic approaches to understanding consequences it will be problematic. Option 3 should be used for all medium and high consequence systems in all medium or large enterprises.

Basis

Small businesses have little choice but to let change happen and use backups to revert and reentry for things not covered by backups. The cost of change control is too high for most small businesses to afford and the systematic approach required is only justified in small business with high tech focus or small businesses in the software writing arena.

Some change management system will be required in order to track changes in any substantial enterprise because there are so many of them and their impacts can be so widespread. For example, any change to a system potentially alters its properties with respect to risk aggregation, so all of the elements of risk aggregation analysis should be performed for any change that has the potential for impacting other systems. Without a systematic approach, a separate analysis will have to be performed for every change, mostly rehashing the previous analysis performed on all of those systems that interact with the changed system. The enterprise should therefore track all of the interdependencies associated with each system so that changes can produce incremental changes to only the systems impacted by the change.

A second major problem is identifying which changes meet risk management concerns. Because incremental small changes can produce rather large overall changes and because of the amplifying effects of interdependencies and risk aggregation, the consequences of change are not always obvious.

The third option is most desirable but it also takes some time to achieve, so most enterprises use a mix of options 2 and 3. The cost of change management can also be substantial so it is typically only used in medium and high consequence systems where the consequences of failure to track changes are far higher than the cost of doing so.

Sound change control implies:

- a system for requesting, specifying, implementing, testing, and implementing changes,
- a method for tracking and backing out changes,
- separation of duties between research and development, testing, change control, and operations,
- databases that track these different elements of the process,
- approval processes and work flows to assure operational execution,
- integration of changes into the detection and response process to prevent false positives and potentially harmful responses,
- notification of audit so they can adapt their auditing to meet the new requirements,
- updated documentation to reflect operational changes and user changes,
- training to adapt the people to the changes,
- HR and legal approval of changes impacting those areas, and
- policies, standards, and procedures must be followed along the way.

The extent to which enterprises go down this path depends on their level of maturity in information technology, the protection program in place, and executive management understanding of the criticality of change management to enterprise operational continuity.

Summary

Change management goes to the heart of large scale information technology deployments and a systematic approach is necessary as enterprises grow.

Security standards: Which ones should I use?

Issue

Which of the widely used enterprise security control standards are best suited to my enterprise?

Options

Options include: (1) GAISP, (2) ISO17799:2005, (3) COSO, (4) CoBit, (5) CAISWG, (6) BS7799, (7) ITIL, (8) NIST SP400-11, or (9) other standards that are industry specific.

Decision

For most businesses, the best combination is Options 1, 2, 3, and 9; GAISP, COSO, ISO17799:2005, and industry-specific standards. Option 6 replaces option 2 if you are in the UK. Option 5 is not harmful but not comprehensive enough to justify its use without other standards and fully encompassed by other recommended standards. Option 7 only applies to select service industries and is not as good as options 2 or 6 in those industries. Option 8 is aging rapidly and option 2 covers it and more. Option 4 serves only to appease auditors, which is beneficial, but it is a poor enterprise selection because it fails to focus on critical enterprise issues.

Basis

Control standards are often considered fundamental to enterprise information protection because they (1) mitigate risks associated with failure to meet due diligence, (2) provide relatively comprehensive coverage so as to avoid obvious missteps and missed areas of import, (3) they reduce the time and effort in defining protection programs, and (4) they are widely accepted so that they are more likely to be accepted by management. The also exist at different parts of the space, covering executive responsibilities (E), management controls (M), and technical operations (T). Mapping this into the standards provided above, we have the following table:

Std/Why	GAISP	ISO	COSO	CoBit	CAISWG	BS7799	ITIL	NIST	Other
Diligence	✔	✔	✔	✔		✔	✔	✔	✔
Comprehensive		✔				✔			
Efficient	✔	✔	✔			✔	✔		✔
Accepted	✔	✔	✔	✔		✔	✔	✔	✔
Coverage	EM	EMT	E	T	EMT	EMT	MT	T	N/A

Standards that are industry specific should be embraced when they are also efficient and accepted. National Institute of Science and Technology (NIST) special publications are generally pretty good but in the security area they are out of date and not well maintained compared to International Standards Organization (ISO) standards. The Information Technology Infrastructure Library (ITIL) is too limited in its coverage to be really useful and it is largely comprised of references to British Standards Institute (BS) standard BS7799, and not even the newest version of that. As a result, while it has substantial acceptance among information technologists because of their use of the other elements of the ITIL approach, it is unwisely embraced as adequate when in fact it is not adequate at all.

BS7799 and ISO17799 are very closely linked to each other. ISO17799 grew out of BS7799, and BS7799 continues to be updated ahead of ISO17799, which ends up being the globally embraced version of BS7799. For that reason, ISO17799 is preferred except for entities limited to the United Kingdom. Following BS7799 is still a good idea, because it will keep you up to date. ISO17799:2005 is substantially better than all of the previous versions and enterprises using previous versions should update.

The Computer and Information Security Working Group (CAISWG) is worthwhile as something to look at but it is too new to be embraced substantially and it has limited coverage and limited utility. The Control Objectives for Information and Related Technology (CoBit) has an enormous amount of backing among the information technology audit community but is highly technical in its orientation and is too dogmatic in ignoring the wisdom of the ages that has been put into ISO17799 and BS7799. It is useful for dealing with auditors, but it would be better to get an auditor who knows how to deal with the better standards.

The Committee of Sponsoring Organizations (COSO) of the Treadway Commission standard is explicitly included in the regulatory interpretation of the Sarbanes-Oxley Act and is by far the best commonly known and accepted approach to enterprise risk management, as far as it goes. The Generally accepted Information Security Principles (GAISP) standard is the universally accepted top level requirement for information protection and should be embraced by all.

Summary

The best selection is a combination of GAISP, COSO, ISO17799:2005, and other industry specific standards for larger entities. Subsets of these should be used for smaller entities.

Your decisions

Your decisions are summarized in the following pages. Enter the decisions you made for each area where you have made a security decision and use these sheets as summaries of your security decisions and as elements of your enterprise security architecture.

Your business

Indicate here the business characteristics you have relative to security decisions:

Characteristic	Yours
Business size: tiny / small / medium / large / huge	T / S / M / L / H
Geographic distribution: local / regional/ national/ global	L / R / N / G
Risk levels encountered: High / Medium / Low	H / M / L
Regulations: Heavy / Moderate / Light	H / M / L
Technology focused with technical expertise	Y / N
Strong risk management program in place	Y / N

Improving security: What's a good first step

Check the steps you now take and that you now want to take.

Selection	Now	Desire
Do a rapid risk assessment		
Do a protection posture assessment		
Do an external information technology audit		
Do nothing		

Defining Risk: How should I define risk levels?

Check the steps you now take and that you now want to take.

Selection	Now	Desire
analyze everything in terms of financial numbers,		
Use a 3-level system defining low, medium, and high risks,		
Use a 10-level system rating risks from 1 to 10.		
Don"t rate risks.		

Spam: How should I handle it?

Check the steps you now take and that you now want to take.

Selection	Now	Desire
Remove individual employee email addresses from web sites and similar public areas.		
Refuse to accept email from large-volume spam sources.		
Scan incoming email for known spam content and remove it.		
Select an ISP that has good spam blocking as part of their service.		
Use commercial antispam products internally.		
Refuse to forward spam email.		
Don't allow internal email lists to work from external sources.		

Spyware: How should I handle it?

Check the steps you now take and that you now want to take.

Selection	Now	Desire
Move away from Windows on the desktop.		
Ignore spyware for low consequence systems and focus on medium and high risk systems.		
Block spyware at a gateway device.		
Block spyware on Windows desktops.		
Disable Windows functions that spyware exploits.		

Wireless: How should I handle network access?

Check the steps you now take and that you now want to take.

Selection	Now	Desire
Don't allow wireless access		
Put wireless access on separate firewalled network segments		
Use Wired Equivalent Privacy (WEP)		
Use Wi-fi Protected Access (WPA) to secure wireless		
Treat wireless access like remote access.		

Firewalls: What kind should I use?

Check the steps you now take and that you now want to take.

Selection	Now	Desire
No firewall is used.		
A network address translation (NAT) firewall is put in place.		
A demilitarized zone (DMZ) area is used for servers.		
Multiple firewalled areas used to separate areas.		
Personal firewalls are placed on select computers.		

Concealed networks: When should I use them?

Check the steps you now take and that you now want to take.

Selection	Now	Desire
Never use deceptions.		
Use deceptions when they are built into existing systems.		
Use deceptions at firewalls.		
Use deceptions within internal networks.		
Use deceptions within systems.		

Background checks: When should I do them?

Check the steps you now take and that you now want to take.

Selection	Now	Desire
Never do background checks on employees.		
only check backgrounds on new employees.		
only check backgrounds for key employees.		
check all employee backgrounds.		

Switches or hubs: Which should I use?

Check the steps you now take and that you now want to take.

Selection	Now	Desire
Use hubs exclusively.		
Use switches exclusively.		
Use switches in most places and have hubs sporadically based on cost limits for upgrades.		

Penetration testing: What is it good for?

Check the steps you now take and that you now want to take.

Selection	Now	Desire
Never penetration test.		
Test when there is an incident and it is desirable to detect the presence of similar vulnerabilities or residuals of the attack.		
Test periodically.		
Test when systems are changed or installed.		
Test during protection assessments.		

Open or closed source: Which is better for me?

Check the steps you now take and that you now want to take.

Selection	Now	Desire
Only use closed source software,		
Only use open source software.		
Ignore this as an unimportant issue.		
Use a mixed strategy.		

Security awareness: What should my plan be?

Check the steps you now take and that you now want to take.

Selection	Now	Desire
Initial awareness training for all employees.		
Periodic security reminders.		
Guest lectures.		
Training sessions.		
Verified learning systems.		
Scenario-based policy awareness programs.		

Disaster recovery: How should I do planning?

Check the steps you now take and that you now want to take.

Selection	Now	Desire
No disaster plan is or should be in place.		
Backup copies of critical data in a media safe.		
Off-site copies of backups and a tested process for getting things going again.		
A pre-arranged set of computer resources available for use in a short time frame.		
Multiple sites with redundant operational capabilities.		

Passwords: How often should we change them?

Check the steps you now take and that you now want to take.

Selection	Now	Desire
Never change passwords,		
Change passwords when there is a specific reason to do so.		
Change passwords at convenient system changeover times.		
Change passwords at regular intervals.		

Remote security: How do I do user access?

Check the steps you now take and that you now want to take.

Selection	Now	Desire
Firewalls for home user computers.		
VPNs or other encryption between home and office systems.		
Dial-in access using telephones and modems.		
Firewalls that identify authorized home use.		
Don't allow home-based access to internal systems.		

Threats: How do I respond to computer extortion?

Check the steps you now take and that you now want to take.

Selection	Now	Desire
Pay the extortion amount.		
Call law enforcement.		
Call an outside expert for emergency assistance.		
Handle the technical issues internally.		

Encryption: When should I transmit encrypted?

Codify your existing transmission encryption decisions:

Sensitivity	Location	Low Risk	Medium Risk	High Risk
all	internal			
all	external			
sensitive	internal			
sensitive	external			

Codify your desired transmission encryption decisions:

Sensitivity	Location	Low Risk	Medium Risk	High Risk
all	internal			
all	external			
sensitive	internal			
sensitive	external			

Encryption: What should I store encrypted?

Codify your current stored encryption decisions:

Location	Low Risk	Medium Risk	High Risk
servers			
local			
mobile			
backup			
primary			

Codify your desired stored encryption decisions:

Location	Low Risk	Medium Risk	High Risk
servers			
local			
mobile			
backup			
primary			

Incident detection: How should I detect attacks?

Enter current and desired decisions into the following tables: (1) wait till consequences reveal attacks, (2) examine log files for detection, (3) automate collection and analysis of logs, (4) use IDS products, (5) use network-wide IDS and analysis, or (6) detect event sequences with potentially serious negative consequences.

Network size	Expertise	Low risk	Medium risk	High risk
small	low			
small	high			
big	low			
big	high			

Desired:

Network size	Expertise	Low risk	Medium risk	High risk
small	low			
small	high			
big	low			
big	high			

Incident response: Who you gonna call?

Check the steps you now take and that you now want to take.

Selection	Now	Desire
Do nothing,		
Use internal people only.		
Call a private detective.		
Call a technical security firm.		
Call law enforcement.		

Security costs: How much should it cost?

Check the steps you now take and that you now want to take.

Selection	Now	Desire
Take a minimum-cost legal compliance approach.		
Take a comprehensive risk management approach.		
Decide to emphasize security as a key company priority.		
Don't budget in advance for information protection, spend on a reactive basis when needs occur.		

Threats: Who would really try to attack me?

Check the steps you now take and that you now want to take.

Selection	Now	Desire
Ignore threat assessment and make guesses.		
Use the Web and other sources to search out information about real security incidents against companies like yours.		
Get a vendor to do a comparative study of similar companies.		
Get a high quality highly directed threat assessment done by an investigative professional.		
Get a high quality general threat assessment done by threat assessment professionals.		

Backups: What should I back up and how often?

Check the steps you now take and that you now want to take.

Selection	Now	Desire
Never backup anything.		
Backup critical information when you feel concerned about losing it.		
Backup everything periodically.		
Create and maintain different backup processes and schedules for different information based on its criticality.		
Continuously and automatically backup everything all the time.		

Backup retention: How long should I keep them?

Check the steps you now take and that you now want to take.

Selection	Now	Desire
Retain backups forever,		
Retain different backups for different fixed periods.		
Retain backup data based on a business value assessment.		
Don't worry about retention periods.		

Backups: How and where should I store them?

Check the steps you now take and that you now want to take.

Selection	Now	Desire
Store in a closet or storage room.		
Store in the computer room.		
Store in a standard business safe.		
Store in a media fire safe.		
Store in off-site storage.		

Security consultants: When should I use one?

Check the steps you now take and that you now want to take.

Selection	Now	Desire
Never bring in an information security consultant.		
Bring them in to provide expertise you don't have.		
Bring them in when you are short on available time to get the security tasks you need to do completed.		
Bring them in for an objective outside opinion.		
Bring them in for political or personal expediency.		

Security policy: How much of one do I need?

Check the steps you now take and that you now want to take.

Selection	Now	Desire
No security policies at all.		
Acceptable use policies.		
Legal and regulatory related policies.		
A wide array of standards-based and other policies.		

Network zones: How should I zone my network?

Check the steps you now take and that you now want to take.

Selection	Now	Desire
No zone separation.		
Several zones for different business functions.		
Many small zones for individual projects.		
A small number of zones and subzones for risk disaggregation.		

Zone	Have	Want	Zone	Have	Want
Internet			Sensitive		
Demilitarized			Restricted		
Business			Control		
Partner			Audit		

Network zones: What should I put where?

Check the steps you now take and that you now want to take.

Selection	Now	Desire
Put systems with like data together and people with like jobs together,		
Put systems with similar risk profiles together and people who have to use those systems together,		
Put Internet-accessible systems in a DMZ, most systems used every day by direct user contact in a business zone, back-end machines in a more restricted zone, highly sensitive or critical data in a more restricted zone, network control systems in a control zone, and audit trails in an audit zone, and		
Limit zone content based on management specified risk management thresholds associated with the protective measures in use.		

Data center redundancy: How many do I need?

Check the steps you now take and that you now want to take.

Selection	Now	Desire
A single data center well protected from all identified threats.		
Two data centers, a primary and a backup,		
More than two data centers distributed across the regions where the business functions.		

Backup facility distance: How far should I go?

Check the steps you now take and that you now want to take.

Selection	Now	Desire
No distance requirement.		
At least 5 miles away.		
In another city.		
At least 250 miles away.		
On another continent.		

Detection and response: How fast should I be?

Check the steps you now take and that you now want to take.

Selection	Now	Desire
As fast as possible.		
As slow as I can be without causing a great deal of harm.		
Detect things that have obvious impacts and respond to them based on available resources and business impact.		
Detect and respond in time to mitigate potentially serious negative consequences.		

Risk aggregation: How do I control it?

Check the steps you now take and that you now want to take.

Selection	Now	Desire
Do ad-hoc risk aggregation mitigation when designers happen to notice the issue or when events drive you to it.		
Analyze aggregated risk for systems that have obvious business criticality.		
Do a periodic risk aggregation analysis and mitigate problems on a scheduled basis.		
Fully integrate risk aggregation into operations and change management practices.		

Change management: How should I handle it?

Check the steps you now take and that you now want to take.

Selection	Now	Desire
Just let change happen and keep backups in case you have to revert to them.		
Create a system to identify and track changes larger than a particular management-defined consequence level.		
Apply sound change controls.		

Security standards: Which ones should I use?

Check the steps you now take and that you now want to take.

Selection	Now	Desire
Generally Accepted Information Security Practices (GAISP)		
International Standards Organizations ISO17799:2005		
Committee of the Sponsoring Organization of the Treadway Commission (COSO)		
Control Objectives for Information and Related Technology (CoBit)		
Computer And information Security Working Group (CAISWG)		
British Standards Institute BS7799		
Information Technology Infrastructure Library (ITIL)		
National Institute of Science and Technology (NIST) SP400-11		
Other standards that are industry specific.		

Summary and your questions

This document attempts to summarize a great deal into simple decision processes. While these decisions are not right for all circumstances, they are often right for the circumstances identified. The object of these decisions is not to make judgments for you, but rather to help you think about decisions in a different light and to inform you of the ways others have thought about these decisions. If they bring something up that has otherwise been missed, there is a benefit to them. And if they give you ammunition for a change, that's fine as well. In the end, you have to make your own decisions for your own enterprise, but hopefully these example decisions provide the information you need to make better and more informed decisions.

Upcoming Decisions

Upcoming articles for Security Decisions tentatively include:
- Where should the CISO function be in the organization chart
- Content control – keeping bad things out
- Content control – keeping good things in
- Fail safe – but when is what safe?
- When should I transfer risks?
- When should I avoid risk?
- When should I accept risk?
- When should I mitigate risk?

Fill in the ones you want and email them to us at http://all.net/

The Market Space

The market space describes what can be bought to aid in the development and operation of the CISO function. It generally identifies 6 levels at which services or products are useful. The depiction of the space here provides a top-level overview of the uses of product and services. The top level is executives under which is project management in all cases. Next there is the mechanism of control used by management, which is often the people who carry out the operations function. The point of impact (the user) comes next then the thing that the user uses, and finally the critical underlying mechanisms or issue.

Policy Standards Procedures	HR Legal	Risk	Testing & Change Control	Technical Safeguards Physical Information	Incidents	Audit	Knowledge and Awareness	Document
Executive ✓	Executive ✓	Executive ✓	Executive	Executive ✓	Executive	Executive ✓	Executive ✓	Executive ✓
Mgmt ✓✓	Mgmt ✓	Mgmt ✓	Mgmt	Mgmt ✓	Mgmt ✓	Mgmt ✓✓	Mgmt ✓	Mgmt ✓
Developer ✓✓	Process ✓	Operation ✓✓	Process ✓	Admins ✓✓	Process ✓✓	Practices ✓✓✓	Program ✓✓✓	Process ✓
Workers ✓	People ✓✓	Analysts ✓	Testers ✓	Users ✓✓✓	Responders ✓✓✓	Auditors ✓✓✓	Students ✓✓	Authors ✓
Rules ✓	Tools ✓	Tools ✓	Tools ✓✓	Systems ✓✓✓	Technolog ✓✓	Tools ✓✓	Teachers ✓	Repository ✓✓✓
Aides ✓	Laws ✓	Basis ✓✓	Fault models ✓✓	Bits&Byte ✓✓✓	Methods ✓✓	Standards ✓✓✓	Curricula ✓	Tech ✓✓

The marks (✓) indicate the level to which this area is presently covered in the marketplace. No mark means that no tools exist at all. A single check mark means that there is expertise and tools available. Two check marks (✓✓) means that the market is settled and there are adequate resources available. Three check marks (✓✓✓) indicates too many products and people in the market and too large a diversity without adequate clarity to make good decisions unless you can get around all of the hyperbole. Thus the ideal situation is the ✓✓ in which the market is settled, pricing is reasonable, competition works to keep prices and features suitable, but dramatic change is not present so decisions can be made for a longer term investment and snake oil salespeople cannot survive.

The market has some major holes and tends to be focused heavily today around the technical tools to support technologists addressing very specific issues. Inadequate tools are available to hep decision makers make good decisions. Testing and change control is given short shrift, but this market is filling up. HR and Legal are under-served as are most of the low level support tools and top level aspects of governance and all of the executive level.

Your notes

Your notes

Printed in the United States
95310LV00003B/48/A

9 781878 109385